The Campus History Series

SOUTHERN OREGON UNIVERSITY

The graduating class of 1904 is gathered to plant a sequoia tree on the old Southern Oregon State Normal (SOSNS) campus, which was located about a mile south of the present Southern Oregon University (SOU) campus. Valuing sustainability has a long tradition at SOU. (Courtesy Southern Oregon University Archives.)

ON THE FRONT COVER: The Southern Oregon State Normal School junior class of 1926–1927 is pictured in front of Churchill Hall. (Courtesy Southern Oregon University Archives.)

COVER BACKGROUND: Southern Oregon State Normal School opened on its new campus in September 1895, with classes held in the newly constructed building on the left. The administration building on the right was completed in December 1903. (Courtesy Southern Oregon University Archives.)

The Campus History Series

SOUTHERN OREGON
UNIVERSITY

MARY JANE DERMOTT CEDAR FACE AND
MAUREEN FLANAGAN BATTISTELLA
FOREWORD BY DR. LINDA SCHOTT, PRESIDENT

ARCADIA
PUBLISHING

ISBN 978-1-5402-4039-2

Published by Arcadia Publishing
Charleston, South Carolina

Library of Congress Control Number: 2019937713

For all general information, please contact Arcadia Publishing:
Telephone 843-853-2070
Fax 843-853-0044
E-mail sales@arcadiapublishing.com
For customer service and orders:
Toll-Free 1-888-313-2665

Visit us on the Internet at www.arcadiapublishing.com

We dedicate this work to the students, staff, and faculty of yesterday, today, and tomorrow: to those who walked the halls of Churchill, who danced in the Britt Ballroom, who fought in the wars and returned to learn, to those who stand against the tide, who work for equality and social justice, and to those who have yet to know this place.

Students are at the heart of Southern Oregon University and its mission. Hard work in recent years to prepare for changing demographics, respond to regional needs, and establish partnerships ensures that SOU is sustainable and will flourish in coming years. Pictured here are student Raider Ambassadors, who provide tours and assistance to new and prospective students. (Courtesy Southern Oregon University Archives.)

CONTENTS

FOREWORD

As a high school student in a small town in Texas, I had a fabulous history teacher who helped me understand how our past informs our future. I became fascinated with the subject and went on to get undergraduate and graduate degrees in history. All that I learned has informed my work as a leader in higher education, deepening my understanding of social dynamics, cultural change, and political struggle. Now, however, I find myself thinking much more about the future, and especially the future of higher education. How will institutions such as Southern Oregon University, formed in a very different time, move into a rapidly changing future?

Since 2017, SOU has been thinking hard about this question and has redesigned it vision, mission, and values. We are even more student centered, regionally engaged, and intentionally drawn than in our past. We know that the success of today's SOU students and those of tomorrow is dependent on our willingness to boldly innovate as we create and re-create SOU as a "university for the future."

Our forward-facing and future-ready focus is possible because of our awareness of the past, both successes and challenges. It is this awareness that allows us to understand the imperative for change that we face today and are certain to experience in the years to come. From the university's earliest days, challenges have propelled Southern Oregon University to respond and lead. In 1869, the community's support and financial contributions led to the opening of the Ashland Academy 1872. Throughout our history, this regional support has made the difference, time and again, between stasis and success. In every era, Southern Oregon University has adapted to the needs of our region and our students, as you will see through the photographs and narratives from our history.

Today, SOU faces more rapid change than ever before. New technologies and new types of learners challenge us to rethink our traditional ways of learning and working, and environmental shifts pose threats to our beautiful region. We acknowledge these difficulties and lead confidently into our evolving future, and we do so informed by a deep understanding of our history.

Thank you for wanting to understand our past more fully. I hope you will enjoy what you learn from these pages, and I invite you to join with us as we prepare for our future.

—Pres. Linda Schott

ACKNOWLEDGMENTS

The historical record can be dry and fact-based, but the story of Southern Oregon University (SOU) is anything but. Our research was richly textured and rewarding, revealing stories, circumstances, and personalities that give life and breath to Southern Oregon University.

Many helped with this project, but the authors would particularly like to thank the following for their photographs, memories, financial support, and encouragement. Without you, this work would be sorely lacking.

Emeriti faculty and staff provided some of the institutional memory we'd lost to time. Many taught during the chaos of the 1960s, coped with retrenchments, and experienced the growth of academic programs firsthand. They could tell us of changes in infrastructure, technologies, and partnerships over the years. Faculty and staff had long memories of even earlier days and earlier generations and assisted us in selecting key events to cover in the work. Many had photographs and ephemera from their time at Southern Oregon University. The keen minds and recall of our faculty and staff identified places, names, and stories that gave the photographs texture and brilliance.

For support and encouragement that make this book possible, we thank university president Linda Schott; Janet Fratella, vice president of development; Matt Sayre, athletic director; Jeff Gayton, university librarian; and the Friends of Hannon Library.

We owe a big thank-you to past and present photographers and curators of SOU photographs, William Stoughton, Tony Boom, and Greg Martin. We also appreciate the many individuals, both on and off campus, who generously provided photographs and contextual information: Thomas Arce, Mike Beagle, Roxane Beigel-Coryell, Christopher Briscoe, Chava Florendo, Mary Gardiner, Riah Gooding, Josh McDermott, Mike Oxendine, Terry Skibby, and others who contributed in ways large and small.

Staff and faculty, past and present, shared stories that informed our work. Special thanks go to Ron Bolstad, Claude Curran, Jim Dean, Sally Rushing Jones, Tom Knapp, Jim McNamara, Tom Pyle, Rich Rosenthal, and Chris Sackett.

For early reads, edits, and encouragement, our thanks go to Ed Battistella, Ron Bolstad, Karen Menzie, and Tom Pyle.

Previous histories of our university by Homer Billings, Arthur Taylor, Roy McNeil, Vaughn David Bornet, and Arthur Kreisman were invaluable.

Mary Jane McDermott Cedar Face thanks Southern Oregon University and her colleagues at Hannon Library for a sabbatical term that gave her time for research and writing.

Unless otherwise indicated in captions, images in this book are from the Southern Oregon University Archives.

INTRODUCTION

Many people know of Southern Oregon University's (SOU) first building in 1872, a square clapboard schoolhouse adjacent to Ashland's Methodist church, where Briscoe School now stands. The school was built by 14 congregant families, was called the Ashland Academy, and was run by a Methodist minister, Rev. Joseph Henry Skidmore.

In 1895, the school was renamed Southern Oregon State Normal School (SOSNS) and was located about one mile south of the present campus on land donated by the Carter Land Company. The parcel of land on old Highway 99, or Siskiyou Boulevard, was then outside the city limits between streets that would become known as Beswick Way and Hillview Drive and across from Normal Street, a street that took its name from the school.

Buildings from the SOSNS campus no longer exist, and few people are aware of that early location. Sepia photographs are left to tell the story of these days—of administrators, faculty, and students in formal dress, in classrooms, on the stage, on the athletic field, and in dormitories. Imagine our surprise at finding a 1905 survey of the SOSNS campus showing street names and locations of classroom buildings, bike paths, a barn, dormitories, a racetrack, tennis courts, and a windmill. Property lines of adjacent lots follow the football field and reveal an orchard and brickyard. Most marvelous of all, there are trees marked on the survey map, and today those same trees are mighty indeed, over 100 years old.

Finding the 1905 survey map made us mindful of Southern Oregon University's continuum of service to the region. SOSNS was an early and important facility to train teachers and educate the youth of Southern Oregon. Those trees shaded music and elocution classrooms and walkways between buildings. Today, these trees protect homes and shelter wildlife. To us, the old football field and bike path in the survey were wonderful harbingers of today's championship athletes and a symbol of Southern Oregon University's contemporary focus on sustainability, health, and wellness.

Strong presidents and expert faculty have always led the way at Southern Oregon University. We pay special attention in this work to Pres. Julius Alonzo Churchill, who served from 1926 to 1932. Southern Oregon University's first building, in its third and present location on Siskiyou Boulevard, is named in his honor.

Under Pres. Walter Redford, the school became an accredited four-year school in 1939. Elmo Stevenson's long leadership gave structure and permanence to the university, and under his administration, the first graduate programs were authorized. The wars brought thousands back to Southern Oregon demanding an education, and Southern Oregon University worked hard to meet their needs.

In every era, Southern Oregon University students have learned new ways of living, thinking, and doing business. This was true in the 1890s, when the Rogue Valley's growing population demanded educators; in the 1950s, when new business paradigms emerged; in the 1980s, with the advent of personal computing; and later, as the campus expanded to Medford and regional partnerships were forged that gave strength and opportunity to Southern Oregon University.

As of 2019, SOU has grown to a head count of over 6,000 enrolled students and offers 36 majors and select graduate programs. The Ashland campus covers 175 acres, and the Higher Education Center serves students in Medford. SOU graduates have made their marks nationally and internationally. A few of the school's notable graduates include Ty Burrell, Emmy Award winner for his role as Phil Dunphy on ABC's *Modern Family*; Paulann Petersen, Oregon poet laureate; Mark Helfrich, offensive coordinator for the University of Oregon Ducks football team; Virginia Linder, the first woman elected to the Oregon Supreme Court; Michael Finley, past national park superintendent and president of the Turner Foundation; Michael Geisen, 2008 National Teacher of the Year; and Juan Carlos Romero Hicks, former governor of Guanajuato and current federal senator in Mexico.

Southern Oregon University has always and will continue to respond to the needs of the region and takes great pride in doing so.

In researching and writing this history of Southern Oregon University, our goal has been to bring forth the stories of people, places, events, and cultural eras that may have been forgotten in the dust of time. With retirements and the passing of generations, institutional memories dim and files and photographs are lost or forgotten. A backward glance can be colored by personal experiences that reinterpret an idea, event, or circumstance. The historical record can, at times, marginalize some stories and experiences and unexpectedly celebrate insignificant details.

As archivists and librarians, we know the importance of remembering and the importance of facts and documentation. We are reluctant to lose the history of Southern Oregon University. We are determined to reveal what can easily become an unknowable past and equally determined to keep that past alive for future generations.

In just these few pages, we hope to tell the stories of faculty and staff and the stories of the students who later made their way in life armed with learning gained in the halls of Southern Oregon University. We wanted to become familiar with some of the relationships forged at SOU among administrators, faculty, staff, classmates, and members of student groups. We wanted to learn about students who pushed their physical limits on the athletic fields and courts of the university, those who would find their vocation and avocation on the stage, and those who learned to become future leaders through campus involvement.

Our task was complicated not only by the physical limits of the printed page but also by the collections available to us. While we had surprisingly good coverage of the university's earliest eras, we had only a few hundred images from the 1940s when, after World War II, the student body doubled in one semester as our boys returned home. After reviewing print photographs from the 1960s and 1970s in the university archives, we came across boxes containing thousands of unprocessed negatives. It was exciting to scan, index, and describe these images that added depth and complexity to our coverage of a remarkable era of cultural change.

We were fortunate to have other resources for researching photographs and their historical contexts. The *Siskiyou*, Southern Oregon University's student newspaper, has been published continuously since 1926 (switching to online-only in 2012) and provided background information about people, places, and events. We also relied on university yearbooks, catalogs, commencement programs, and other university records for verifying names and dates. Even within standard publications like university yearbooks, gaps exist, because some have been lost to time or were never published. The final yearbook was published in 1992, and so that annual time capsule is no longer available. We only came across one extant yearbook from the Great Depression years, a homemade scrapbook dated 1930. The *Ashland Daily Tidings* and the *Medford Mail Tribune* were also invaluable in pinpointing dates and names and presenting facts and context about photographs.

Many of the images and sources, including university yearbooks and catalogs, that we used during this project were previously scanned and available on Hannon Library's online Southern Oregon Digital Archives (SODA). Established in 2000 with funding from the federal Institute of Museum and Library Services (IMLS), the growing SODA online resources provide a rich collection of images and textual documents that give depth and breadth to SOU and regional history. As we progressed through this project, we scanned and described hundreds of additional images as we found them, and they will eventually be added to our digital collections, commemorating those who came before and providing a significant resource for anyone curious to learn more about Southern Oregon University's history and unique story. For the many people, places, and events we are not able to include in this work because of space limitations, we are working hard to preserve and make this important history available in the Southern Oregon Digital Archives. Regardless of whether one is a serious researcher or a casual browser, SODA collections provide a gateway to viewing images from SOU's past and its campus.

We expect you'll enjoy this book and its brief excursion into the past as much as we did while researching and writing the work. It's a window to the history of Southern Oregon University and a door to its future.

In order to best appreciate Southern Oregon University's long history, it is helpful to document the official names of the institution. Prior to 1895, Southern Oregon University had a variety of names that were inconsistently used in newspapers, catalogs, programs, correspondence, and official records. In some cases, appellation varied within the same document. There were also several commercial schools in Ashland that were not antecedents of the university but have at times been confused with it. For these reasons, we offer here the formal and most consistent names from official documents beginning at the university's official inception in 1872.

Southern Oregon University's name changes are documented as follows: Ashland Academy, 1872–1882; Ashland State Normal School, 1882–1895; Southern Oregon State Normal School, 1895–1932 (closed 1909, reopened 1926); Southern Oregon Normal School, 1932–1939; Southern Oregon College of Education, 1939–1955; Southern Oregon College, 1956–1974; Southern Oregon State College 1975–1996; and Southern Oregon University, 1997–present.

One

EARLY DAYS

Southern Oregon University can trace its beginnings to 1869, when local citizens formed the Rogue River Valley Educational Society with the goal of building an academy of higher learning. Funds were raised through subscription sales, a building lot was donated by A.D. Helman, and construction of a new building began. Despite the group's hard work, funds were insufficient to complete the building. Under new leadership of the Reverend Joseph Skidmore, who obtained a mortgage, the building was completed, and the Ashland Academy opened in November 1872. Because of continuing financial problems, the Methodist Episcopal Church took over the academy in 1878.

In 1882, the Oregon legislature authorized creation of a state normal school in Ashland for teacher training, and the school was renamed Ashland State Normal School (ASNS). Unfortunately, state funding did not accompany official authorization as a normal school. Financial woes continued, and over the next several years, the school was operated by the Methodist Episcopal Church and various individuals and groups, including a private association of Ashland citizens who had purchased shares in the school and attended regular ASNS stockholder meetings.

The institution was renamed Southern Oregon State Normal School (SOSNS) in 1895 and held classes on a site about a mile south of the present campus on land donated by the Carter Land Company. In 1899, the state assumed oversight of the college; the legislature approved funding and established a board of regents. By 1903, the college was the state's largest normal school, with 270 students. The school continued to struggle financially even as the student body and course offerings grew.

The state legislature failed to fund Oregon's normal schools in 1909, and the board of regents closed Southern Oregon State Normal School. Local citizens donated enough money so that the students could finish out the school year. Citizens then began a long campaign to reopen the normal school, including lobbying, state ballot initiatives, and speaking to groups about the need for teacher training in Southern Oregon. Their efforts were ultimately successful when, more than 15 years later, the legislature reauthorized both a normal school in Ashland and its funding.

In autumn 1872, Ashland Academy, the earliest incarnation of Southern Oregon University (SOU), opened as a combined primary, secondary, and higher education institution. A Methodist Episcopal Church committee was charged with raising funds. Unsuccessful at fund-raising, contributors and the church turned the project over to Rev. Joseph Henry Skidmore and his wife, Annie Hill Skidmore, who completed the building and opened the school on North Main Street, where Briscoe School now stands.

The class of 1885 is shown under a sign that reads, "The Reward of the Faithful Is Certain." There were two graduates this year (in front, left to right), Martha Russell (Boyd) and Amanda Goodyear (Eubanks). Five juniors are standing behind the graduates, from left to right: Emma Vining (Winkler), Jessie Plumerth, Doria Russell (Walter), Dora Anderson (Wight), and Allen Simon. One individual is unidentified.

By 1886, Ashland was a growing, bustling city. In this picture, stagecoach and wagon drivers assemble on the plaza. On December 17, 1887, Charles Crocker, the vice president of the Southern Pacific Railroad Company, drove in the golden spike in Ashland that formally connected the two tracks coming from the north and south, connecting Oregon to California. (Courtesy SOU Hannon Library, Stories of Southern Oregon digital collection.)

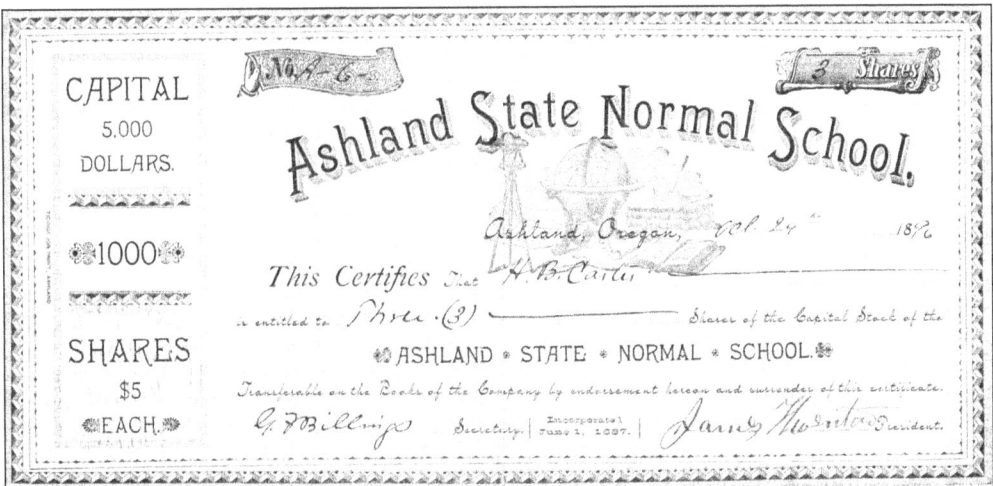

The Ashland State Normal School was incorporated on June 1, 1887, and funded by stockholders who purchased shares in the school. This is a receipt for three shares at $5 each for H.B. Carter, dated October 24, 1896, and signed by corporation officials G. Billings, secretary, and James Thornton, president.

Stockholders met regularly, usually at the Ashland Woolen Mills. Minutes from the stockholders meeting on June 17, 1892, show elections to the board of regents. Stockholders present included W.H. Atkinson, D.R. Mills, J.M. McCall, G.F. Billings, James Thornton, F.H. Carter, E.K. Anderson, W.H. Leeds, Jacob Wagner, W.C. Myers, H.B. Carter, and E.N. Carter.

F.H. Carter, pictured here, was a stockholder and member of the ASNS Board of Regents for many years. The Carter family and Carter Land Company were strong supporters of the school, donating the land for the normal school campus. The Honorable E.V. Carter helped secure the first and succeeding state appropriations for the school.

In 1895, W.T. Van Scoy became president of the newly renamed Southern Oregon State Normal School (SOSNS). That fall, there were 133 students, and the school's eight faculty were paid an average of $200 per year. In 1899, the Oregon legislature made its first appropriation of $7,500 for the biennium. Van Scoy served as president, an elected position, until 1900, when W.M. Clayton was elected.

Alice Applegate served as principal of the SOSNS Training School from 1888 to 1890, when only unmarried women could be faculty members. Alice was the granddaughter of pioneer Lindsay Applegate, who blazed the southern route of the Oregon Trail, known as the Applegate Trail. Alice later married Emil Peil and lived on Granite Street in Ashland. Alice organized the Ashland Study Club, which helped bring the Chautauqua to Ashland.

The new campus of Southern Oregon State Normal School opened in 1895 with the academic building pictured here and a women's dormitory. Community members worked to establish the school by contributing funds and land. The seven-and-a-half-acre campus was located near the intersection of present-day Normal Street and Siskiyou Boulevard, a mile south of today's campus.

An early graduate in 1896, Susanne Homes Carter dedicated her life to teaching and in 1920 was elected superintendent of Jackson County schools, serving for 12 years. When visiting rural schools, Homes drove with her horse tied to the back of her car. If roads got rough, she completed the journey on horseback. Susanne Homes Residence Hall was later named in her honor; today, the building has limited use.

Benjamin F. Mulkey served as SOSNS president from 1902 to 1907. In his first year, enrollment jumped to 270 students, and training school enrollment was capped at 76 children. SOSNS was the largest normal school in Oregon. Enrollment growth strained resources, including transportation for commuters. One morning in September 1902, fifty-six people were counted waiting at the corner of Main and Pioneer Streets for the three-and-a-half-mile wagon ride to campus.

With funding from a legislative appropriation, a second building was completed in December 1903 and called the Administration Building. The building contained the library, classrooms, science laboratories, the president's office, and reception rooms. There was a gymnasium with adjacent showers, dressing rooms, and physical culture rooms. The library held 1,500 volumes.

This photograph of a girls' dormitory room was taken in 1904. A head of the girls' dormitory was charged with maintaining a wholesome and refined environment. Dormitory rooms were furnished with a bed, bedsprings, table, chairs, fuel, and lamps. Students were required to bring their own bedding and mattress or mattress ticking. Students washed and ironed their own clothes in the washhouse, using the stove, boiler, and washtubs.

Student escapades are rarely documented, but this photograph, dated October 1, 1904, tells the story of students who walked "to town" to celebrate the New Year, returning about 12:15 a.m., well past the 9:00 p.m. curfew. The girls were locked out of their dormitory and entered through Ida Robinson's room, breaking a mirror. A faculty meeting and discipline followed, though history fails to record the students' punishment.

The teacher training program began in 1895, but it wasn't until 1899 that the program had its own building. There were classrooms for Ashland children in grades K–9. The training school brought Ashland children to campus and prepared SOSNS students to become teachers. Enrollment of children in the teacher training program reached a high of more than 100 students during the 1903–1904 school year.

Student teachers who taught in the SOSNS Training School in 1903 are, from left to right, (first row) Floy Cambers, Raymond Bates, Ola Mickey, Clyde Briggs, and Aura Thompson; (second row) Delia Tibbetts, John Tyler, Andrew Warde, George Milam, Docia Willetts, and ? Tuttle; (third row) Lou Grubb, Loleta Norton, Lela O'Hara, Eva Storey, and Walter McIntire; (fourth row) George Marksbury, unidentified, Herman Anderson, Victor Vallely, Lillian Perceful, Donna Bell, and Lucie George.

19

The class of 1907–1908 was one of the last training school classes before the closure of Southern Oregon State Normal School in 1909. This photograph of children, student teachers, and instructors captures a special moment in the history of the SOSNS "model school."

The Glee Club is pictured in 1905. Shown are, from left to right, (first row) Worth Harvey, Goldwin Herndon, James Fairclough, Frank Shelley, and Ernest Wright; (second row) Herman O. Anderson, DeWitt Goodpasture, James A. Martin, Obie H. Newton, Kay V. Loosley, Carl Richardson, and Fred L. Neil. Other student associations that year included Debating Club, Moot Senate, Athletic Association, European Club, Shakespearean Club, Historical Society, and literary clubs.

20

Armilda Doughty's general history class is captured in this January 1905 photograph. Doughty also taught economics and geography. By 1905, the Southern Oregon State Normal School faculty had grown to 12, including normal school president Benjamin F. Mulkey, who taught psychology and pedagogy. Courses were offered in six broad areas: science, history, civil government, athletics, arts, and manual training.

1910

1085 — SOUTHERN PACIFIC DEPOT, ASHLAND, OREGON.

SOSNS students from Oregon and Northern California were able to come by train to Ashland, arriving at the Southern Pacific Depot. The Ashland Depot Hotel is pictured here. Train access provided Ashland with an advantage over other towns of Southern Oregon, contributed to the growth of local industries including milling and orchards, and helped bring the Chautauqua program to Ashland. (Courtesy SOU Hannon Library, Stories of Southern Oregon digital collection.)

The Southern Oregon State Normal School bus, pictured here in 1905, was affectionately called "Black Maria," the slang term for a hearse. Each year, R.P. Neil supplied horses for the carriage free of charge. Students were able to travel to and from the train station and between downtown Ashland and the campus. This image is from an undated postcard addressed to Gertrude M. Deierlein.

This photograph of the Ashland Chautauqua building was taken in the early 1900s, before the building was enlarged in 1905. The Chautauqua movement came to Ashland in 1893 and faded away in the 1920s. With a goal of furthering moral and intellectual culture, Ashland Chautauqua programs consisted of concerts, classes, prayer meetings, and lectures. (Courtesy SOU Hannon Library, Stories of Southern Oregon digital collection.)

The football team, pictured here on March 8, 1897, includes players from Ashland and the normal school. The team had just defeated Eagle Point in a game played in Central Point. Years later, during 1902–1903, SOSNS improved the football grounds, built bleachers, and hired a coach, W.B. Scott, who had been a quarterback for the University of Oregon. The SOSNS team played teams from other universities and high schools.

SOSNS's strong athletic programs extended to women's athletics and the 1905 basketball team pictured here with coach Clyde Payne. At the time, there were two men's and two women's basketball teams. SOSNS also offered baseball, lawn tennis, football, track, walking clubs, and a fencing club.

The SOSNS men's basketball team of 1905 is, from left to right, (first row) James A. Martin, Herbert Eastman, and Bert Samuel Stancliffe; (second row) Clyde A. Payne (coach), Ernest Wright, Ernest J. Smith, Kay V. Loosley, Herman O. Anderson, Alfred Willard Scullen, and Charles Murphy.

The men's track-and-field team is pictured in 1905. Included in this photograph are, from left to right, (first row) Goldwin Herndon, Edwin McKillop, Fred W. Bagley, and Alfred Willard Scullen; (second row) C.M. Bailey, Frederick C. Homes Jr., Alfie Cole, Bert Samuel Stancliffe, James A. Martin, ? Anderson, Leonard Smith, ? McIntire, Frederick L. Peterson, Edward W. Pollard, Clyde A. Payne (coach), and Howard Carmichael.

The graduating class of 1908 had 27 students—5 men and 22 women. In 1908, the SOSNS campus was made up of several buildings, including the academic building, administration building, training school, and men's and women's dormitories. There were 15 faculty, including the president, Benjamin F. Mulkey. One year later, SOSNS closed when the state legislature failed to authorize funding.

On May 1, 1909, May Day was celebrated with a maypole dance. In this picture, the SOSNS May Queen, Nelle Lewis, is seated on a dais, surrounded by her attendants and others, including children, who took part in the maypole dance. On either side of the gathering are uniformed men holding spears.

25

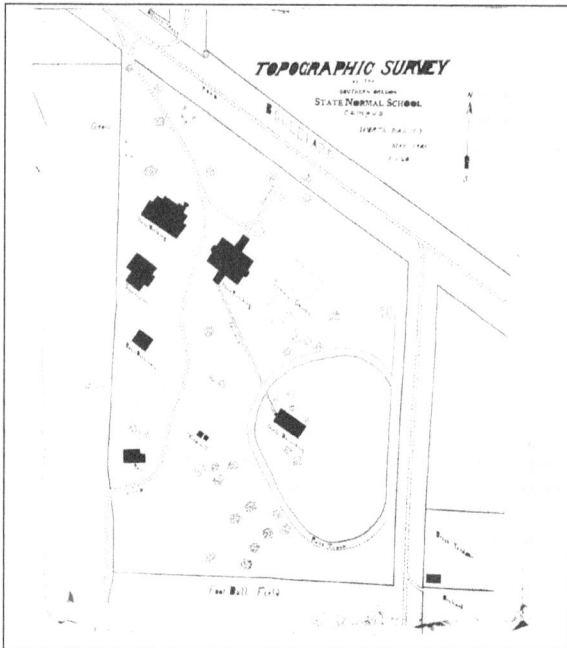

This topographic survey map, created by Worth Harvey and dated May 1905, shows the layout of the old SOSNS campus on Siskiyou Boulevard at Normal Street. Directly behind the two main buildings, which face Siskiyou Boulevard, is the gymnasium. The boys' dormitory is behind the gymnasium, while the girls' dormitory is separated from it by a long sidewalk. The survey also shows tennis courts, a windmill, and a barn.

This is a picture of the SOSNS campus shortly before it closed in 1909, when the state legislature failed to fund Oregon's normal schools. This photograph was used on promotional postcards that local citizens created as part of their long campaign to reopen the normal school. Around this time, efforts, which never came to fruition, were also made to open a University of Southern Oregon in Medford.

Two

New Beginnings

Following the closure of Southern Oregon State Normal School by the Oregon Board of Regents in 1909, the region united to advocate for a teacher training school in Southern Oregon. In 1925, after years of lobbying, fund-raising, presentations, and bills introduced in the state legislature, $175,000 was appropriated for a normal school building, and an ongoing millage tax ensured maintenance. Sen. George W. Dunn, from a local pioneer family, introduced and shepherded the bill. The City of Ashland donated 24 acres for a new campus, the present site of SOU.

Construction was completed on the building now known as Churchill Hall, and SOSNS officially reopened on June 21, 1926, with a summer session. A dedication event was held later that week. Speakers included Oregon governor Walter Pierce, University of Washington president Henry Suzzalo, and other dignitaries.

Like other Oregon normal schools, SOSNS was administered by a board of regents. The board appointed Julius Alonzo Churchill, state superintendent of public education, to serve as president. Churchill quickly hired new faculty, including Marion Ady (art), Helen Anderson (English), Verne Caldwell (psychology), Pearl Durst (librarian), Walter Redford (geography), Arthur S. Taylor (history), and others.

The SOSNS course of study was a state-standardized, two-year program; 96 credits were required for graduation. All students were expected to comply with a code of conduct that demanded high social and ethical standards. Student teaching opportunities were provided in Ashland's Lincoln Training School in coordination with the Ashland School District.

Despite the Great Depression, SOSNS grew programs in an attempt to maintain enrollment. In 1932, the school name was officially shortened to Southern Oregon Normal School (SONS). President Churchill left to serve as president at Oregon Normal School in Monmouth and director of Oregon's elementary school programs. The same year, Walter Redford was appointed SONS president, and the normal school expanded into a junior college offering more courses and evening classes.

In 1939, after the Oregon Board of Regents eliminated normal schools, SONS received full accreditation from the American Association of Teachers Colleges. After the school received accreditation, Oregon governor Charles Sprague signed a bill changing the institution's name to Southern Oregon College of Education.

This is a photograph of the Ashland Plaza in the mid-1920s, providing a glimpse of Ashland during the years when Southern Oregonians advocated for the reopening of a regional college. This goal was realized when Southern Oregon State Normal School opened in 1926.

Julius Alonzo Churchill was appointed the first president of the soon-to-open SOSNS in 1926. Having served as state superintendent of schools and in other positions, Churchill brought a wealth of experience. He quickly hired 12 faculty to teach in the normal school as well as 10 women to teach in the nearby teacher training school, and he set the school's curriculum.

When Southern Oregon State Normal School opened its doors on June 21, 1926, all classes were held in the new Administration Building, now known as Churchill Hall, named after Julius Alonzo Churchill, president from 1926 to 1932. Among the first faculty members were Marion Ady (art), Arthur S. Taylor (social science), and Wayne W. Wells (science). This is a view of Churchill Hall before landscaping.

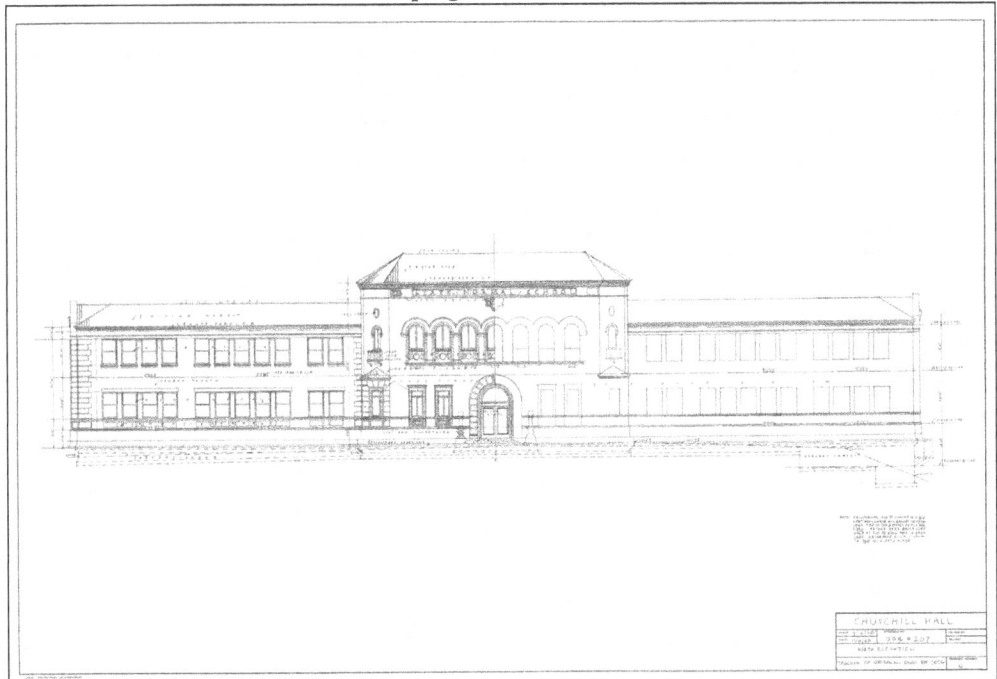

This blueprint shows the north elevation of Churchill Hall, which was built on the 24-acre campus donated by the City of Ashland. The building, then called the Administration Building, housed all classrooms, the library, and administrative offices. Construction of Churchill Hall began in 1925 with a state appropriation of $175,000, of which $5,000 was set aside for developing the grounds and $5,000 for library books.

A gargoyle on the facade of Churchill Hall is an example of the Italian Renaissance style featured throughout the building, which at the time seemed suited to Southern Oregon's Mediterranean climate. The architects were John V. Bennes and Harry A. Herzog from Portland, Oregon. The Churchill Hall architectural plans were subsequently used by Eastern Oregon University to construct its administration building. (Courtesy Terry Skibby.)

Faculty and administrators are pictured outside Churchill Hall during the 1926–1927 academic year. From left to right are (first row) Margaret Cason, Lillian Nicholson, Marion Wilson, and Clara Trotter; (second row) Vern Caldwell, Pearl Durst (librarian), Eva White, Georgia Mooney, Elizabeth Richardson, Martha Wattenbarger, Beatrice Hall, and Edith Bork; (third row) Wayne Wells, Bertha Stephens, Virginia Hales, and Marion Ady; (fourth row) Arthur Taylor, Arthur Strange, Mattie Hileman, Walter Redford, Katharine Vincent (registrar), Helen Anderson, Leona Marsters, and Pres. Julius Alonzo Churchill.

The junior class of 1926–1927 is pictured in front of Churchill Hall. At the time, tuition was set by the state at $6 per term; student fees of $3 and a health service fee of $1 brought quarterly costs to $10. The normal school course followed a standardized two-year certification program that included student teaching.

Science Club members and advisors from 1926 to 1927 are pictured here. The club's purpose was to promote interest in science and in the natural surroundings. Faculty advisers were Walter Redford, Wayne Wells, and Verne Caldwell.

Members of Theta Beta Phi, a sorority, are pictured here. The goal of the sorority was the advancement and encouragement of scholarship. From left to right are (first row) Jane Pollard, Florence McPhillamey, Edith R. Deuel, Naomi Gray, Cecil McCracken, and Verna B. Hogg; (second row) Ida Grace Morris, Letta C. Eastburn, E. Lovely Harris, and Hazel Edmiston.

Belle Headlee graduated in the SOSNS class of 1928 and remained active in the SONS alumni association. More recently, the Belle Headlee Hewitt '28 Endowed Scholarship was established by her son, Roger G. Hewitt, to provide educational opportunities for deserving graduates from Medford, Oregon, high schools who attend Southern Oregon University.

32

Male and female students participated in the normal school marching band, as seen in this undated photograph taken in front of Churchill Hall around 1930. The marching band included brass, woodwind, and percussion instruments.

Members of the SOSNS "O" Club, presided over by Prof. Francis Neff, are responsible for the letter O placed on the hillside northeast of Ashland around 1930. Quartz-like rock was crushed by sledgehammers and used to create the letter. Supplies were hauled with a team of mules and a wagon.

The letter *O* on the hillside northeast of Ashland is being painted for the first time. Prof. Walter Redford, who later became president, is pumping. Leroy Huntley is holding the spray can level, and Jack Feeny is spraying. (Courtesy Jack Feeny.)

An SOSNS group is visiting Crater Lake. Early SOSNS promotional materials extolled Ashland's natural surroundings. The 1926–1927 catalog notes, "The wooded canyons, the tumbling streams, the silver lakes, the snow-capped peaks make a veritable playground and offer many delightfully interesting trips. . . . In any easy day's journey may be visited the Oregon Caves, Lake of the Woods, with its guardian Mt. McLoughlin, Crater Lake, Klamath Falls, and Klamath Lakes."

Roy T. McNeal is pictured with an SOSNS geology class on a field trip to Mount Lassen in Northern California. The class climbed the 11,000-foot summit and then went down into the crater to study geologic formations of the volcano, which last erupted over the years 1914–1917.

Oaks Pharmacy in Ashland in 1930 advertised its sale of "Normal Textbooks" in the large side window. Dr. Francis Gustavus Swedenburg, who had offices above the pharmacy, lived near campus in what was then called the Swedenburg House and later the Plunkett Center, which now serves as the offices for the SOU Foundation.

This photograph was taken on Spring Campus Day in the 1920s, a day off from classes and an annual day of service that also often included faculty vs. student games and a barbecue. From left to right are Jean Stratton, Prof. Francis Neff, Rosalind Wise, Jack Feeny, Mamie Timmons, and T-Bone Caldwell. (Courtesy Jack Feeny.)

In 1926, Lincoln Training School was built on Siskiyou Boulevard, across from the Ashland High School, for $42,280, of which SOSNS contributed $20,000. Ashland School District purchased the lot in 1922 for $6,300. Lincoln was staffed by SOSNS students and graduates and managed by the college, although the school district set the calendar and standards for attendance and student conduct. The college and school district shared the cost of teacher salaries.

Second-grade students in the Lincoln Training School are shown painting a replica of the Ashland Springs Hotel as part of a social studies project in which students created a scale model of the city of Ashland. The photograph was taken during the 1931 summer session.

Elementary students enrolled in the Lincoln Training School are pictured in front of the school in 1931. Lincoln School contained 8 demonstration rooms and 20 classrooms. Eventually, the school became fully part of the Ashland School District. Lincoln School closed after the 2004–2005 academic year because of Ashland's changing demographics and declining enrollment.

Taking the helm when President Churchill left for Oregon Normal School at Monmouth, Walter Redford served as the president of SONS from 1932 to 1946. Redford first taught geology as one of the early faculty hired in 1926, and after he moved into the presidency, coach Roy McNeal taught geology in his place. This photograph of Redford was taken long after retirement in 1971.

Three male Southern Oregon State Normal School students and one faculty member are pictured in 1929 enjoying the nice weather and appearing quite relaxed. From left to right are Henry May, Prof. Francis Neff, Orville Wilson, and Lyle Kenney.

Angus Bowmer joined the SOSNS faculty as an English teacher in 1931, when the school only offered one course on play production in the teacher training curriculum. Bowmer quickly added courses on lighting, scenery building, and costuming in addition to producing a play each spring. Bowmer played Shylock in Shakespeare's *The Merchant of Venice* in 1934 and founded the Oregon Shakespeare Festival in 1935. This photograph of Angus Bowmer is from 1970.

This photograph, taken around 1930, shows a grove of madrone trees on the site where Britt Hall now stands. The photograph of madrones west of Churchill Hall was taken facing north, with Oregon Highway 99 (Siskiyou Boulevard) in sight beyond the trees.

First named Memorial Court, Britt Hall was the second building constructed on the current Southern Oregon University campus. It was completed in 1936 at a cost of $45,000 and remodeled as Britt Hall thanks to a significant contribution from Mollie Britt's estate. The most recent remodel was in 2010, and today, Britt Hall is home to the Enrollment Services Center, other administrative offices, and the communication program.

In this aerial view of the SOSNS campus and surrounding Ashland streets in 1941, it is easy to spot Churchill Hall and Britt Hall. The next decades would bring more construction to the campus.

Three

WAR YEARS, BOOM YEARS

The Great Depression hit Southern Oregon hard, and by 1939, Southern Oregon College of Education (SOCE) enrollment was declining. By 1941, most male faculty had joined the military, and men who otherwise might have gone to college enlisted as well. In 1941, President Redford started up a two-year secretarial program and an associate degree in merchandising to encourage female enrollment, but only 59 students enrolled in the fall 1945 term. There were no yearbooks or student newspapers, and athletic programs were put on hold as the country waited out the war and waited for its boys to come home.

And come home they did in the fall of 1946, when 387 men enrolled as freshmen, bringing the student body to 492. Clubs, societies, and sports started up with a roar, and the 1946 football team won every game. The next year, 1947, saw the return of both the yearbook and the *Siskiyou* student newspaper, student reporters writing with manic energy. Every dorm and academic discipline had its elected student leadership, and the Greeks flourished. College life was vigorous and exciting, as older and more mature students transformed the campus culture. Omar's opened in 1947 as an almost on-campus beer joint serving fried chicken dinner for just $1.25. Babies naturally came along, and almost every day it seemed the *Ashland Tidings* announced new parents with a Veterans Village address.

The 1950s was an era of major capital expansion, as new construction tried to keep ahead of enrollment. Dormitories, classrooms, and service buildings were erected in months, and the construction of McNeal Pavilion in 1957 finally gave athletics a proper home. Campus infrastructure was improved, as massive tunnels for central heating connected the campus so that the old boilers in each building could be taken out of service. By 1959, student enrollment had reached 1,259, and Pres. Elmo Stevenson was planning ahead for 10,000 students over the next decade. Stevenson recommended property acquisitions and expanded the campus borders across Siskiyou Boulevard in a 20-year plan that was approved by the Oregon State Board of Education.

The 1938 Civilian Aeronautics Training Act funded four Oregon programs, including SOCE, University of Oregon, Oregon State University, and Multnomah College in Portland. SOU's physics instructor, Dr. Winifred Bradway, would provide ground training, and Thomas A. Culbertson, the Medford Municipal Airport superintendent, would teach flight. Seventy-five students would complete training through SONS before the program was suspended in 1942.

ORE-V-35358, Ashland   Oct. 23, 1940
#4. View from point about 30' north of NE corner of Bldg No 4 of upper row looking SE. Shows rear entrance Bldgs Nos 1, 2 and 3 of upper row.

The boys came home from World War II in September 1946, and student enrollment skyrocketed. Housing was as important as classrooms, so Veterans Village was constructed in October 1946. Seven buildings housed four apartments each and were assigned to families of veterans; the eighth building had accommodations for 64 single male veterans. The buildings were moved to the North Campus and renamed College Court in 1957 in preparation for the constructions of the new Commons building.

Susanne Homes Residence Hall was constructed in 1947 as a dormitory for 84 female students. The building had a cafeteria that served 250 students, a living room, and a recreational area where dances and other student events were held. In this 1953 photograph, both male and female students are enjoying a newspaper fight. Snow-covered mountains are seen through the big bay windows.

The H-shaped Pine Hall—also called Science Hall—was constructed in 1947 from surplus war buildings to house the new science programs, a lunch counter, the bookstore, and classrooms. In this 1947 photograph, students are working at lab benches. The college's science and math programs were enhanced in 1940 as a military-preparedness initiative.

Students crowded into Pine Hall for a quick lunch, as shown in this 1948 photograph. Adjacent to Pine Hall was the Student Union, also known as the Siskiyou Shack because it housed the student newspaper and a student buyer's cooperative. These two military surplus buildings, Pine Hall and the Student Union, were located where the Hannon Library is today. Pine Hall had many uses over the years into the 1990s.

The library on the first floor of Churchill Hall was packed in 1948. There were 20,848 books and bound periodicals in the library that year, and interlibrary loan services made the collections of all state libraries available to Southern Oregon College of Education. Overdue fines were $1 per day at the discretion of the librarian, Myrtle Funkhouser, who was first hired in 1928.

Angus Livingston Bowmer (1904–1979) came to the Southern Oregon Normal School in 1931 as an English instructor, and he taught until retirement in 1971. After military service, he immediately ramped up the college theater program and the Oregon Shakespeare Festival, which had last staged a production in 1940. Bowmer formally announced an annual Summer Shakespeare Workshop in the SOCE summer 1950 catalog, the antecedent of Margery Bailey's Institute of Renaissance Studies and later the National Endowment for the Humanities–funded summer Shakespeare in Ashland workshops at SOU.

Central Hall was completed in 1951 with funding from state appropriations. The library was on the second floor (and the floors tilt to center today), with a children's library and classrooms on the first floor. The students' radio broadcast studio was in the basement. In this photograph, students are moving books from the earlier library location in Churchill to Central Hall.

Irene Arashiro was the second Hawaiian student (her sister Arlene was the first) at SOCE. She was a sophomore in 1953 living in Susanne Homes Hall. When Irene first laid eyes on tall, handsome football captain Ernest Bretzel, she determined to marry him. Irene was voted homecoming queen that fall, and Ernest was her escort. Irene and Ernie wed in 1954 and celebrated many happy years together.

The year 1952 was all bobby socks, saddle shoes, and modest skirts as students lined up for meals in Susanne Homes Residence Hall. The large bay windows of the living room area looked out over the valley, couples were discovered snoozing in the big soft sofas, and students played the piano and sang songs in the evenings.

46

Goldfish gulping was a college rage in 1939, with students setting records at 101 and more fish swallowed. This photograph shows that the trend was still alive at Southern Oregon College of Education in 1952. This unidentified young man is surrounded by fellow students who look on in amusement and disbelief as he downs a goldfish.

Theta Delta Phi was an honorary men's scholarship society. A district convention of Oregon's chapters was held at Southern Oregon College of Education in May 1954, with 30 delegates from Eastern Oregon, Southern Oregon, and Oregon College attending. This robot oddly celebrates a 100-year future anniversary of the society at Southern Oregon University.

Sadie Hawkins Day was first documented in a November 15, 1937, *Li'l Abner* comic strip, in which the man who lost the race was troth to Sadie, the "ugliest girl in Dogpatch." While in later eras, Sadie Hawkins Day was reenacted as a demonstration of women's empowerment, in this 1953 photograph, it was still a comedy of confusion.

Pres. Elmo Stevenson sits at the console of the Southern Oregon College airplane in this 1956 photograph. Stevenson recruited heavily throughout Southern Oregon and Northern California and often flew into remote areas of the region to spread the good word about Southern Oregon College.

48

The newly built Science Building opened in 1959, with an annex added to the south in 1967. A 2014–2015 renovation provided structural and seismic upgrades, new windows, ADA upgrades, and remodels of student spaces and 25 laboratories. The Science Building currently houses the Division of Science, Technology, Engineering, and Mathematics.

This 1959 photograph is of Arthur Kreisman, hired by Stevenson in 1946 as assistant professor of English/languages. Before retiring in 2002, Kreisman would serve as director of general studies, dean of humanities, dean of arts and sciences, and in other capacities. He was elected to the Ashland City Council and was the first chairman of Ashland Community Hospital's board. Kreisman authored *Remembering, A History of Southern Oregon University*.

This aerial photograph shows the rapid and significant expansion of Southern Oregon College in 1958. Siskiyou Hall, at top right, was completed in the final months of that year, as was the new Science Building, whose footprint is evident in lower right. The Commons and Huffman Hall along Siskiyou Boulevard were completed earlier that year, and the old Ashland Hospital, at lower left with the circular drive, was in use as a men's dormitory; this was later the site of the Stevenson Union. Pine Hall is the H-shaped building towards center, near the Snack Building; both were military surplus buildings moved to campus in 1947. This area shows the former location of Veterans Village. The aerial also shows the college's expansion to the North Campus; McNeal Pavilion was completed in 1957, and Veterans Village was moved near that location and renamed College Court in 1958. The Commons is known today as the Marion Ady Building, and Huffman Hall was demolished to make way for the Schneider Museum of Art.

Pres. Elmo Stevenson holds an ambitious blueprint for the future of Southern Oregon College in this 1959 photograph. His 20-year plan for 10,000 students was well underway by that point, with the completion of Susanne Homes Residence Hall, Huffman Hall, Siskiyou Hall, the Commons, Central Hall, the Science Building, the Britt remodel, and athletic facilities. Approved and yet to come were a second men's dorm; social science, arts, and experimental school buildings; and more athletic facilities.

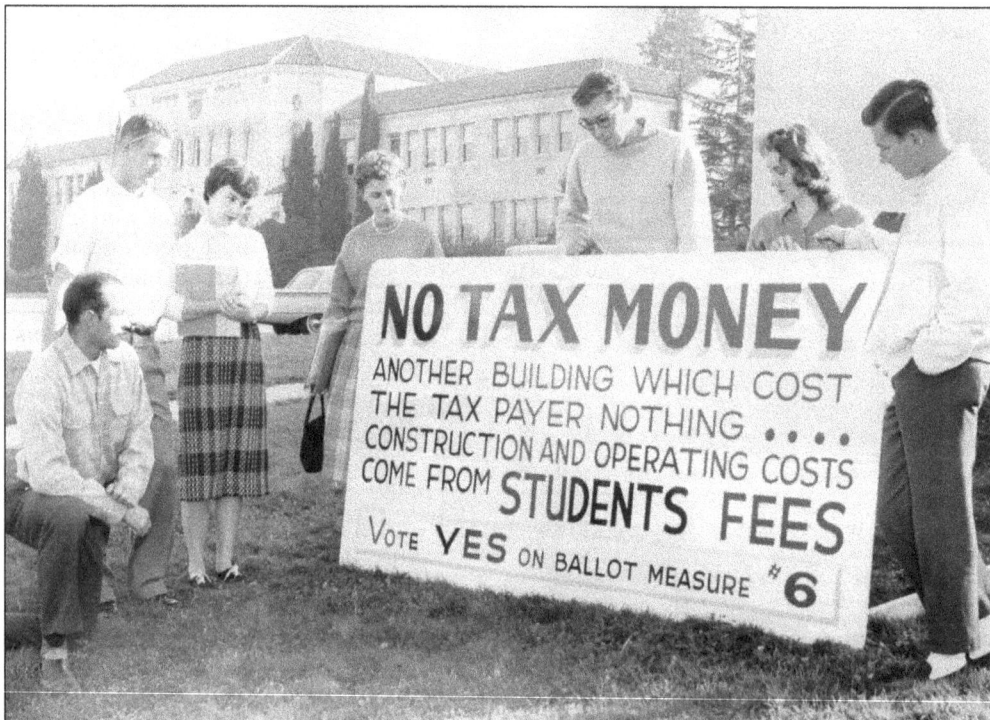

Students defend Oregon Ballot Measure 6 in the 1960 election, which allowed the State of Oregon to increase its bonded indebtedness to construct additional higher education facilities. Their sign, "No Tax Money," acknowledges that Southern Oregon College buildings were funded in good part by student fees, a $5-per-term assessment instituted in the late 1940s that would grow to $12 per term in the 1950s.

Four

CHANGING TIMES, CHAOTIC TIMES

The social and cultural changes occurring nationally and globally in the 1960s and 1970s reached the Southern Oregon College (SOC) campus. This was a time when traditions like homecoming and campus day coexisted with antiwar protests, Earth Day events, streaking, and the alternative Living/Learning Program situated in Susanne Homes Hall. A growing focus on inclusion and diversity was evidenced by the first Las Posadas event in December 1967, the formation of the Black Student Union in 1969, the hiring of a director of minority students in 1970, Indian Awareness Days in 1975, and the creation of a women's center in 1976.

The physical campus was transformed with the construction and opening of new buildings, including the Student Health Center in 1962, Taylor Hall in 1965, and the library in 1967. The Greensprings Residence Hall Complex opened in 1969 on the north side of campus. A student union was constructed, opening in 1972 and named Stevenson Union after past president Elmo Stevenson. During 1966–1967, the Science Building was expanded, and Central Hall was remodeled. Two years later, the KSOR student radio station was established.

Students were not the only group to rebel. In 1966, faculty took a stand when the entire faculty council resigned, feeling ignored by the administration. This led to the development of a new faculty constitution and bylaws, establishment of the faculty senate, and a new governance model.

The college saw significant administrative changes during these decades. Pres. Elmo Stevenson retired at the end of the 1968–1969 school year, with Pres. James K. Sours taking the reins in the fall of 1969. The name of the school officially changed from Southern Oregon College to Southern Oregon State College (SOSC) in 1976. After serving 10 years and dealing with a budget crisis, President Sours retired in June 1979 and was replaced that fall by Natale Sicuro.

Academic programs evolved considerably during this era. Notably, during 1963–1964, the state board granted permission for the school to begin offering graduate programs, approving master's degrees in general studies and business education. A new position, dean of academic affairs, was created to oversee academic programs; this position was filled in January 1978 by Ernest Ettlich.

This is a view of downtown Ashland, near the Plaza, in the late 1960s. Soon after, construction began on the Angus Bowmer indoor theater, beginning the city's shift to a tourism-dominated economy. In the 1970s, Ashland became an eclectic mix of descendants of pioneer families and newer hippie residents who shopped at the Lithia Grocery on the Plaza. The Ashland Food Co-Op was founded in 1971.

Students, faculty, and staff gathered on the football field on April 18, 1963, for the annual Campus Day, a decades-old tradition. Activities included a baseball game, nail-driving contest for girls, tug-of-war, limbo, twist contest, pie-eating competition, races, and performances by music groups including the Travelers Three and the Lettermen. The day included a cookout; students used the bleachers as tables for the meal.

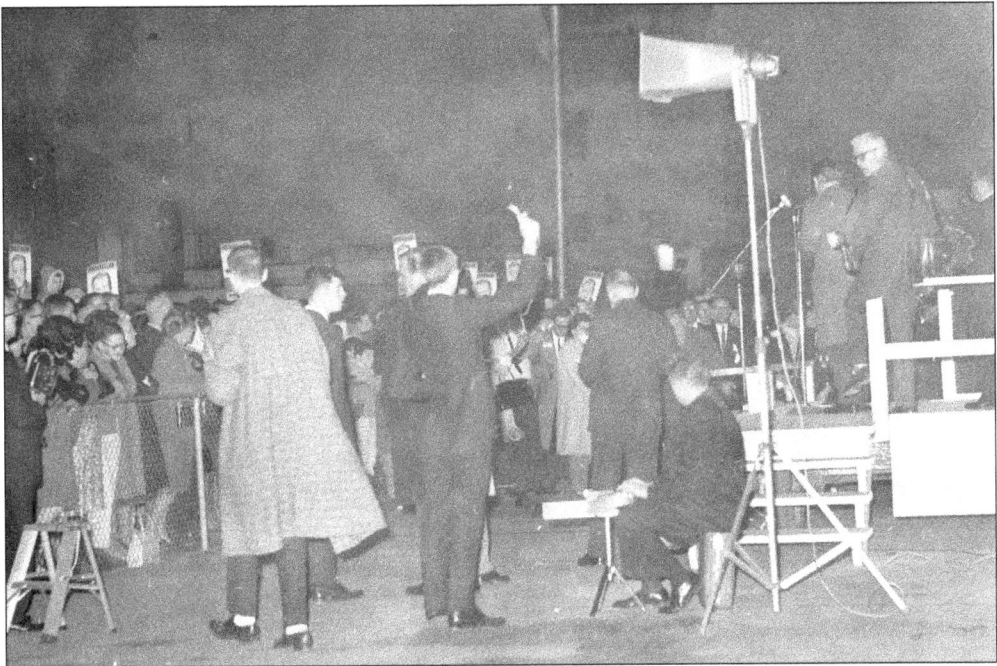

A presidential hopeful on the Republican ticket in 1960, 1964, and 1968, New York governor Nelson Rockefeller visited Ashland and Medford on February 7 and 8, 1964, to rally the Republican vote. Other Oregon towns on the 1964 campaign circuit were Roseburg, Portland, and Salem. SOU students attended the rallies, including this one in Medford.

Taylor Hall was constructed in 1965 to house the social science programs and named for the late Prof. Arthur S. Taylor, who had served as chair of social sciences. Today, Taylor Hall houses several social science programs, including criminology and criminal justice, economics, history, Native American studies, political science, and sociology/anthropology.

Mary Christlieb was a much-loved dean of women and then dean of students at SOC during the turbulent years of the 1960s and 1970s, on occasion bailing students out of jail after arrests for demonstrating. Dean Christlieb oversaw dormitories, the student union, student clubs, advising, and the health center. A supporter of women's rights, she was instrumental in the founding of the Women's Resource Center and Schneider Children's Center.

Hawaiian Club members are pictured in the early 1960s. They are, from left to right, (first row) Sandy Walker, Marion Miyashiro, Linda Seto, Jeannette Ige, Patsy Sunada, Karen Watanabe, Lillian Tanaka, Carolyn Kotsubo, Linda Ikeda, Priscilla Muraoka, and Norma Waki; (second row) Joyce Takenake, Janet Owens, Jim Stauffer, Pearl Hasegawa, Naomi Inoshita, Gail Inoshita, Lorraine Imai, June Matsui, Kako Kondo, Diane Enos, and Marythea Grebner (club adviser); (third row) Theo Chang, Ken Matsumura, Lee Oman, Roger Duvall, Jose Culala, and Dan Buckingham.

This is a photograph of the exterior of the Cascade Residence Hall Complex in the late 1960s. The Cascade Complex opened in 1960 with one residence hall and a dining commons. More buildings were added in 1966. The complex, when completed, included 10 buildings, recreational facilitates, lounges, and computer labs. In 1994, the Cascade Food Court was remodeled and expanded.

In this photograph, a student is studying in her dormitory room in the Cascade Residence Hall Complex. The complex contained 401 dormitory rooms at its height of occupancy and largely closed with the opening of the Raider Village complex in 2013. The buildings still stand today.

Concerts and other events, termed Firesides, were regular highlights of the large lounge area of the Cascade Residence Hall Complex. This Cascade Fireside, which took place around 1970, features the New Prime Minstrels with Ron Kilby.

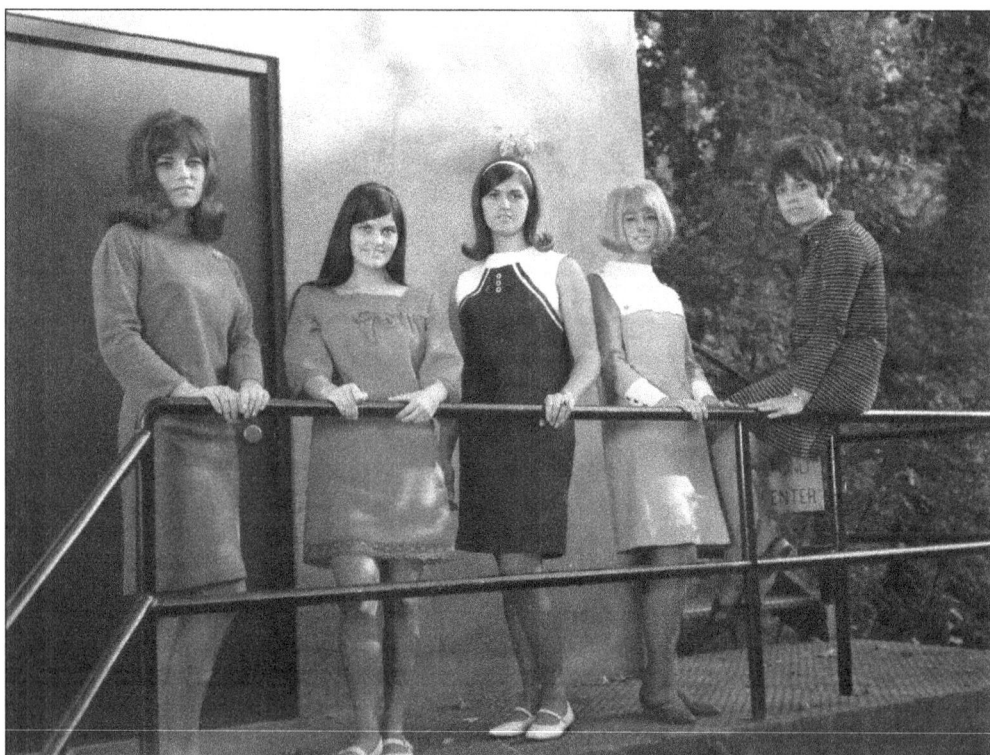

The 1960s and 1970s were a time of turbulent transition as social norms, institutions, dress, social etiquette, and sexual mores were rapidly evolving. Although the era was marked by protest and social experimentation, traditions continued. This is a photograph of the 1967 SOC homecoming court, posed in Lithia Park: from left to right are Sherry Campbell, Carol Shirley, Betty Schwiebert, Laurie Spelgar, and Cathi Morris (queen).

In 1967, the newly built, modern library building opened. The three-story structure had 65,000 square feet and was constructed at a cost of $1.6 million. The up-to-date library had seating for 870 library patrons and housed a reference area, current periodicals room, microform collection, and government publications department. Before the opening of the new building, the library was located on the second floor of Central Hall.

SOU has hosted many Las Posadas events, traditional Mexican celebrations of the Nativity, since the 1960s. This is a photograph of a Las Posadas fete that took place the evening of December 14, 1967, in the McNeal Pavilion gymnasium. The event was organized by Grace "Señora Chela" Tapp-Kochs and sponsored by the Foreign Languages Department.

Students are lounging in front of the Greensprings Residence Hall Complex in the 1970s in this photograph. The Greensprings Residence Hall Complex, which opened in 1969, consists of four dormitories that house 376 students. The complex is still in use today.

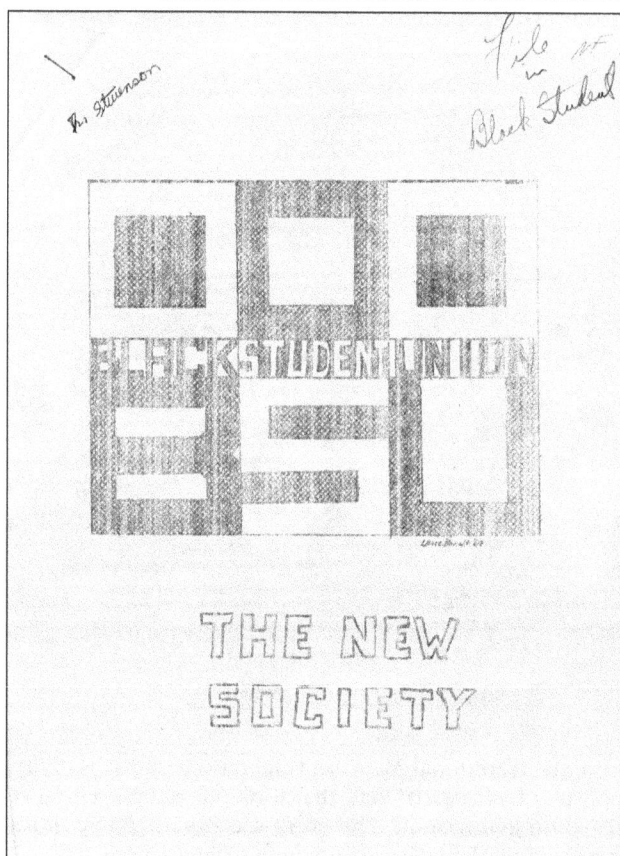

A 1969 pamphlet, *The Black Student Union: A New Society*, explains the goals and programs of this new organization, which was open to all students with a membership fee of $2 per term or $3 per year. Chester McCall served as the first president of the Black Student Union (BSU) and helped organize the weeklong Black Cultural Symposium held in April 1969.

A student deejay from the SOC radio station, KSOR, is pictured here. KSOR was established in 1969 as a tiny 10-watt station formerly led by commercial broadcaster David Allan Borum and expanded with grant funds in 1976 to reach 100,000 listeners. Ron Kramer took over management of the station in 1974, and by 1979, KSOR was building translators to expand its regional coverage and also began carrying National Public Radio programming.

Like other young people around the nation, students at SOC participated in protests against the Vietnam War. This is a picture of the student-organized Peace March that took place on May 17, 1969. Students and a few faculty gathered in front of Britt Hall and marched to the Lithia Park band shell, where this photograph was taken.

Folk singer and labor activist Pete Seeger came to campus in 1969 for a campus symposium called Man vs. Environment. Also in 1969, on October 15, SOC students participated in the national Moratorium to End the War in Vietnam. Demonstrations and teach-ins took place across the country protesting the United States' involvement in the Vietnam War.

James K. Sours was president of SOC from 1969 to 1978. During his 10 years as president, several new academic degree programs were developed, including an interdisciplinary master's program, despite diminished state funding. This photograph was taken in the fall of 1969, during President Sours's first year.

Members of the Black Panthers traveled to the Southern Oregon College campus from the Bay Area. This c. 1970 photograph is stamped "SOU News Service" on the back. (Photograph by Bill Bayley.)

This photograph, dated May 6, 1970, is a close-up in front of Churchill Hall of SOC students responding to the Kent State killings. On May 4, 1970, the Ohio National Guard had opened fire on unarmed Kent State College students protesting the Vietnam War and American bombing of Cambodia, resulting in four deaths. At SOC, flags were lowered to mark the deaths and over 100 students gathered in protest.

63

Pres. James K. Sours greets newly arrived representatives from Dankook University, Pres. Chang Ho-sung (center) and Prof. Dong-Shik Chi (right), at the Medford airport in May 1970. President Sours was instrumental in establishing a sister university relationship with Dankook University in Seoul, South Korea. After his retirement, Sours served as development consultant for Dankook University. Honoring more than 30 years of friendship, two Dankook Awards for Outstanding Undergraduate Students are given annually at commencement.

The Skiesta Prince and Princess for 1970, Rod McNeal and Vivian Rae Brittsan, are pictured here in the 10th annual Ore-Cal Skiesta sponsored by the SOC Mountain Club. The event brought representatives from schools in Oregon, California, and Washington for a weekend of ski competitions, inner tube races, dances, coronation of the queen, and parties.

Mike Smith, student body president, is breaking ground for the new student union building on April 19, 1970; Pres. James K. Sours and Marythea Grebner look on. The original three-story, 84,000-square-foot building was constructed on the former site of the Ashland Hospital and was completed in 1972 at a cost of $3.2 million. It was named Stevenson Union, and the dining area was called Elmo's to honor the late university president Elmo Stevenson.

This is a photograph of the recently completed Stevenson Union. The building was home to student organizations and clubs as well as student government, the bookstore, conference rooms, offices, and the large meeting rooms called the Arena and the Rogue River Room. Renovations over time have added areas for student support programs, the James K. Sours Student Leadership Center, student program offices, and an addition to the relocated bookstore.

During the 1960s and 1970s, there were several honor societies on campus that were an important part of student life; four members of Tri Zeta are pictured here. The purpose of Tri Zeta was to promote campus service, spirit, and cooperation. Members volunteered in many ways—from ushering at plays, lectures, and concerts to helping on blood mobile days and organizing the Klothes Kloset in the basement of Britt Hall.

Pres. James K. Sours and William Maurice Sterling, director of minority students, are pictured in the early 1970s. Presidents Elmo Stevenson and Sours both provided support to students of color in various ways, ranging from tuition assistance to funding for the BSU's Black Cultural Symposium, held April 16–20, 1969. The symposium included movie screenings, panel discussions, arts performances, and a keynote by noted journalist Louis Lomax.

SOU has a long history of serving international students. This is an undated photograph of international students at SOC in the 1970s who were members of the International Relations Club and includes, from left to right, Kako Kondo (Japan), Priscilla Mbuvi (Kenya), Clifford Somkence (Southern Rhodesia), Jose M. Culala (the Philippines), unidentified ,Majid Seifnia (Iran), and Douglas Legg (adviser).

The Music Building, which houses the music academic program and the Music Recital Hall, was built in 1972 at a cost of $1.7 million. The recital hall seats 436 guests and is the preeminent concert hall in Southern Oregon. A pipe organ was installed in November 1974 and named after a donor, Worth Harvey. Additional fund-raising allowed for installation of a practice organ for students and an electronic music lab.

During this era of experimentation, SOC tried new and alternative pedagogical models. For three academic years, from 1972–1973 through 1975–1976, around 120 students participated in the Living/Learning Program housed in Susanne Homes Residence Hall, a coed dormitory. Students lived and learned together and were able to customize their learning experiences, ranging from relatively conventional classes to integrated learning having "no necessary relation to the traditional boundaries of subject matter fields," proclaimed an informational brochure about the Living/Learning Program

Construction of the new 47,500-square-foot Education/Psychology Building was completed in 1973 at a cost of $2.4 million. In addition to classrooms for SOC's psychology and education programs, the building housed the Community Preschool, with an adjacent playground. The preschool served children ages three to five and provided learning experiences for elementary and early-education students at SOC.

SOSC hosted Indian Awareness Days from October 23 to 25, 1975, bringing a group of young people from the Warm Springs Indian Reservation to campus. The group's presentations included dancing exhibitions and a series of lectures. Native artworks were displayed. The weekend began with a tipi raising on the field in front of Stevenson Union. Annual powwows began in the 1990s.

Southern Oregon University began offering specialized programs for foreign-language speakers nearly 40 years ago. This is an early English language class for foreign students. Once called the American Language Academy, SOU's Intensive English Program today helps international students develop the skills necessary to succeed in both American universities and the rapidly changing global environment.

Yvonne Rose-Merkle (left) and Susan Berryhill (right) attend a Women in Transition (WIT) potluck; the organization grew into the Women's Resource Center (WRC). In 1976, Rosemary Dunn Dalton, a nontraditional student, helped establish WIT, funded with a grant written by Mary Christlieb. Dunn Dalton taught the university's first women's studies course and helped found Dunn House, a shelter for battered women and their children.

Long before the Farm, SOSC students were growing plants from seeds and seedlings. Since construction of the Sours Greenhouse in 1980, countless students have purchased plants at the annual spring plant sale. At the dedication on November 2, 1980, the greenhouse was officially named after former SOU president James K. Sours. The cost of construction was $79,000, which was financed with a National Science Foundation grant and by donors.

Five

RAIDER PRIDE

The Southern Oregon State Normal School athletic program officially began in 1926 with the reopening of the campus. What were in the past intramural events, town-gown games, and recreational athletics became competitive team sports, at least for the men. Throughout Southern Oregon University's history, winning coaches and talented male athletes have taken home trophies in football, basketball, wrestling, and track and field.

Digging the footings for the first locker room and laying out the playing field for his athletes, Roy McNeal coached football from 1927 to 1931. Several coaches later, Ashland and Medford High Schools coach Alexander Irving Simpson was called in as a substitute coach in 1943. World War II left Southern Oregon Normal School with few male students, and Simpson returned to high school coaching. His Ashland basketball and Medford football teams won state championships in 1944, and Simpson was named Oregon's Coach of the Year. Simpson's high school games drew crowds of 9,000, and Camp White brought its own bleachers because so many soldiers wanted to watch the game. In June 1946, Simpson was named head coach at the college, and that fall, the football team won 15 consecutive games, including the first Pear Bowl.

Other successful men's team coaches over the years included Al Akins, Bob Riehm, Chuck Mills, Dan Bulkley, and Monty Cartwright, to name just a few. Dozens of athletes competed in and won National Association for Intercollegiate Athletics (NAIA) tournaments, earning national recognition. Beginning in the 1960s, coaches Beverly Bennett, Gail Patton, Shirley Huyett, Sally Rushing Jones, Marian Forsythe, Joanne Widness, and others paved the way for women in competitive athletics at Southern Oregon State College and in the Pacific Northwest.

At first, Southern Oregon State Normal School fields and facilities were rudimentary at best. It was not until 1936 that Memorial Court (later Britt Hall) was built with hardwood floors that would function as both basketball court and ballroom. Dressing rooms and recreation facilities were in the basement. McNeal Pavilion, a two-story building with two basketball courts, a swimming pool, and locker rooms in the basement, was constructed on the North Campus in 1957. The McNeal Pavilion was demolished in 2017, making way for the Lithia Motors Pavilion, completed in 2018.

Roy Wilson McNeal is 31 years old in this 1927 photograph, when President Churchill hired him to build and coach a competitive football team. McNeal, who started successful football programs at Albany College and Puget Sound, was recruited to increase enrollment. McNeal coached from 1927 to 1931, with an overall 13-9-5 record, then taught geography until his retirement in 1972.

The 1931 SONS football team was 3-0-2. In this photograph, Coach McNeal stands to the left, and Claude Hines is in the back, third from the left. An African American student from Bend, Hines was an amateur boxer and excelled in football, baseball, basketball, and track while on campus from 1929 to 1931. Hines is in the Oregon and SOU Hall of Fame.

These women are practicing archery in 1926 at a time when women's athletics were not formally recognized. The first women's intercollegiate sports programs began in 1950 under Beverly Bennett, but it would take Title IX for women's athletics program to gain official status and improved funding.

Jean Eberhart coached football and basketball from 1935 until he joined the US Navy in 1943. He was instrumental in building SONS's intercollegiate athletics program. Eberhart devised a crow's nest placement of referees above the basketball backboard, shown here during a Memorial Court game. The crow's nest was news throughout the country but not adopted elsewhere.

Al Simpson led the 1946 Southern Oregon College of Education football team to victory in the first Pear Bowl, with the team winning 15 consecutive games. Simpson's winning strategy was to unlock the body and the mind with humor and relaxation. Practices were on the hill

Football players Chuck DeAutremont (1948, left) and Thaine "Tex" Gatlin (1950, right) are pictured in 1946. Both were three-sport athletes who played under Simpson in the Pear Bowl. DeAutremont, who was related to notorious mail train robbers Roy, Ray, and Hugh DeAutremont, later signed with the Los Angeles Rams and coached and taught math at Central Linn High School in Oregon. Gatlin's grandson Greer now coaches at SOU.

in front of Churchill Hall, so the team was called "Sidehill Wampus." The 1946 football team is regarded as SOU's winningest team.

Dan Bulkley coached tennis, skiing, and track and field from 1952 to 1978. His track teams won seven conference titles and produced 81 champions. Bulkley was a lifelong athlete and ran a 100-meter dash for his 100th birthday party at RoxyAnn Winery. Dan Bulkley passed away in 2018 at the age of 101.

Beverly Bennett coached women's tennis, basketball, volleyball, track and field, and field hockey teams; taught modern dance; choreographed drama productions; and taught faculty wives' weight-loss classes from 1950 to 1984. She was also the university's first and most ardent advocate for women's athletics before and after Title IX required gender equity in education.

Morris "Morrie" Jimenez (first row, left) was a three-sport athlete and Far West League Conference All-Star in 1952. Jimenez taught and coached football in many Oregon schools and was a lasting advocate for Native culture and language. He served as chairman of the Klamath tribes, was president of the Oregon Indian Education Association, and was Oregon's Title IV (Indian Education Act) coordinator.

Al Akins (left) coached wrestling, baseball, basketball, golf, and football during his tenure from 1955 to 1978. Akins developed an effective and winning football spread offense with frequent passing, based on speed rather than strength. Akins coached women's athletic programs before these were sanctioned by the National Association of Intercollegiate Athletics.

Danny Miles (1965–1968) was a three-letterman at Southern and went on to coach basketball at Oregon Institute of Technology for 45 years. He is known as Southern Oregon University's winningest basketball coach ever and is one of only four SOU coaches with over 1,000 wins. Miles retired in 2016 and was named to the National Collegiate Basketball Hall of Fame in 2018. He currently serves as a Southern Oregon University board member.

77

Until the McNeal Pavilion (pictured here) was constructed in 1957, athletes used Memorial Court facilities (now Britt Hall). A pool, gym, and dance studio were added to McNeal in 1966, and the gym was enlarged in 1991, when athletic offices were relocated to that facility. The McNeal Pavilion was demolished in 2017 to make way for the Lithia Motors Pavilion.

Skiing entered Southern's curriculum in 1950 thanks to Dan Bulkley. He was a founder of Mount Ashland Ski Area in 1964, and he operated a rudimentary lift with his automobile's engine. Bulkley also started Skiesta, an SOU ski festival that began at Mount Shasta in the early 1960s and ended at Mount Ashland in the early 1970s.

Men's coaches for 1967–1968 were photographed during a women's basketball practice. From left to right are unidentified, Bill Holmes, Mike Mendinboro, Dan Bulkley, Lee Howard, Burt Merriman, Larry Dotson, Bob Riehm, Scott Johnson, Gerald Insley, and Gary Nelson. In 1968, after Holmes's team qualified for the National Association of Intercollegiate Athletics (NAIA) basketball championship playoffs for the first time since 1948, he was carried downstairs to the pool and thrown in.

Sally Rushing Jones (second row, standing at right) started out as a temporary women's tennis coach in 1974–1975 and continued on to coach many of the women's teams until retiring in 1998. Jones was a patient, persistent, and cordial activist for women's athletics in the wake of Title IX, when women around the country were losing their jobs for supporting gender equity in sports.

Greg Haga, at 190 pounds, dominated the mat while he was at SOSC from 1982 to 1985 and was a three-time NAIA All-American. Since 1986, Haga has coached wrestling at Crater High in Central Point, where his teams have won eight state championships; he has been voted Oregon wrestling Coach of the Year five times.

Dave Adams controls the wrestling mat in this photograph from 1978, when the wrestling team was coached by Bob Riehm. Riehm was coach from 1969 to 1994 and led the Raiders to 18 NAIA final eight appearances and three national championships. During Riehm's tenure, the Raiders went 270-71-2 in dual meets. He coached 13 NAIA National Champions, and 100 NAIA All-Americans and earned National Coach of the Year honors twice.

Chuck Mills was athletic director and coached football from 1980 to 1988. Mills fostered a relationship with Tomoyuki "Ted" Suzuki of Suzuki Motors. Suzuki served on the SOU Foundation Board and twice took Southern's football team to Osaka, Japan, to play Kwansei Gakuin University; the Japanese team played at SOU in 1986. The Japanese version of the Heisman Trophy is called the Mills Cup.

Gary Prickett (far right) was SOSC's first dean of development and college relations from 1980 to 1989. He also held the posts of athletic director and dean of the school of business and was elected mayor of Ashland, serving from 1975 to 1979. Prickett started the Raiders Foundation, formalizing contributions directed to Southern Oregon State College athletics programs.

Raider Stadium was built in 1983 at a cost of $1.55 million and seats 4,000, with a covered grandstand on the west side of the field. Fuller Field, named for Ashland postmaster John Fuller, has been the home field of the Raiders football team since 1955. The Meyer Fitness Center, which lies under the grandstand, was renovated in 1999 to include a second floor. (Photograph by Al Case.)

This 1980s-era photograph shows three of Southern Oregon State College's women's coaches. From left to right are Sally Rushing Jones, Beverly Bennet, student athlete Cindy Ramsey, and Mary Crawford. Not pictured are coaches Marian Forsythe and Joanne Widness.

Gail Patton coaches a women's basketball game from the bench in this 1985 photograph, but tennis was her passion until retiring in 2008. Patton also coached the Ashland High School tennis team, taught and coached tennis throughout the city of Ashland, and now teaches tennis at a local fitness club and organizes Big Al's Tennis Tournament.

Athletics thrived under Monty Cartwright's leadership while he served as the head track-and-field coach from 1985 to 1998 and athletic director from 1995 to 2001. During this time, athletics had its strongest and longest run of regional and NAIA championships for both individual athletes and teams. Cartwright was a strong proponent of women's athletics and introduced women's soccer and tennis in 1995. He is pictured here in 2006.

Southern Oregon University's men's basketball team plays Oregon Tech at the 1999 Cascade Conference Championship, a home game in McNeal Pavilion. Pres. Stephen Reno admires students painted in school colors; gamewise, it looks like a tense moment.

Shirley Huyett was head basketball coach for the women's teams from 1990 to 2001 and is the winningest coach ever in any sport at SOU, with 300-plus basketball wins. Huyett's teams advanced to conference playoffs every year during her tenure and competed in national tournaments three times.

On Presidents Day, February 22, 1990, coach Sally Jones heard a big thud and ran downstairs to discover that the McNeal Pavilion pool ceiling had collapsed. Then–dean of administration Ron Bolstad says the ceiling supports had rusted out; the pool was unavailable for the rest of the year for repair and asbestos removal. No one was hurt.

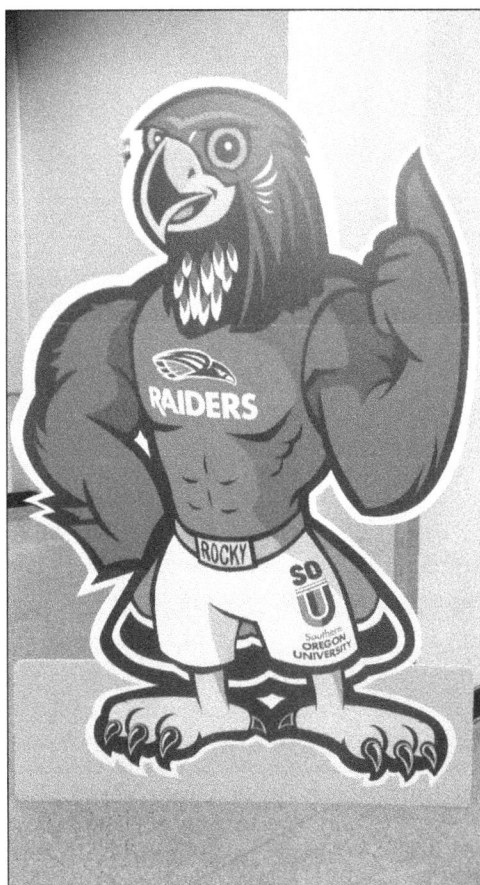

The SOU logo and mascot have gone through numerous incarnations since its inception in the 1950s, not all of which were culturally sensitive. The least appropriate logo and mascot was a cartoon-like red Indian used as late as the 1970s. This red-tailed hawk incarnation was adopted in 1998, but the first version of the red-tailed hawk logo was developed by Native American Student Union member Hans Davis in the mid-1990s.

Matt Sayre came to SOU in 1995 as an offensive assistant for the football program and was named athletic director in 2010. During Sayre's tenure, 10 of SOU's 12 athletic programs have gained national attention. Sayre is pictured with the latest Raiders logo, a contemporary, streamlined hawk that puts earlier, more controversial logos to rest.

The Lithia Motors Pavilion was completed in 2018, greatly exceeding the footprint of the old McNeal Pavilion. The adjacent Student Recreation Center, funded by $17.7 million in fees that SOU students levied upon themselves, features a two-court gym, suspended indoor running track, fitness center, and climbing wall. The facility does not have a pool.

Six

THE ARTS

From dramatic productions and art classes in the earliest buildings to the multimillion-dollar complex known collectively as the Oregon Center for the Arts, Southern Oregon University has a long tradition of arts education, performing arts, visual arts, and the narrative art of the written and spoken words.

The arts programs have had notable faculty and students over the years. Marion Ady taught art from 1926 until her retirement in 1965. Leon Mulling's appointment was in speech, but he exercised a great love for dramatics and funded many student scholarships across the arts. Lyle Matoush in printmaking, Peg Sjogren in painting, Jim Romberg in ceramics, and others—all have left their marks on the university and mentored new generations of artists.

The Music Building was constructed in 1972 under the architectural direction of Hamlin, Martin, Schultz and Oredson. The recital hall is significant for acoustic clouds above the stage that are angled to send sound to the audience and side and back panels angled to diffuse and enhance acoustics. The Rogue Valley Symphony Orchestra, the Southern Oregon Repertory Singers, and other groups also perform to full houses in the Music Recital Hall.

The Music Recital Hall is known as one of the premier acoustic performance spaces in the Pacific Northwest, showcasing the talents of faculty like Terry Longshore, Rhett Bender, and others. Cynthia Hutton is artistic director and conductor of Youth Symphony and Youth Orchestra of Southern Oregon and has received many awards for outstanding service and performance in the arts.

The emerging media/digital arts program uses the new Digital Media Center, where students produce award-winning animation, films, and technology-based cultural products. Rogue Valley Community Television, housed in the same building, supports campus, community, governmental and regional recording, television production, and broadcast initiatives.

Southern Oregon University had a long tradition of performing and visual arts even before the Oregon Shakespeare Festival's beginning in 1935. Prof. Irving Vining taught elocution and oratory in 1896 and was the first of the university's faculty to play the role of Shylock in *The Merchant of Venice*; Angus Bowmer was the second in 1935. Vining and Bowmer's work to bring theater audiences to Ashland and students to the Southern Oregon Normal School set the stage for a future filled with creativity.

Elocution was an important skill in the age of Chautauquas, and Irving Vining was the first to teach the subject at the new college. Vining is Shylock in this 1896 production of *The Merchant of Venice*. He was known as the "silver tongued orator of the northwest" and traveled the country promoting Ashland, returning to open the lavish Vining Theater (long gone) with his brother Robert in 1914.

This early SOSNS theatrical performance took place in 1896. From left to right are (first row) Morton Newton, Lyle Kimball, Irving E. Vining (dramatic coach), Ada P. Thomas, and Rosa Dodge; (second row) Chet Easter, Bernard Spencer, Fred Homes, John Berry, James Storms, and T.W. Miles. Vining also taught literature and elocution, the latter a required course each term taught in two rooms designed for voice culture and special drills.

The Merchant of Venice was staged again in 1905 under the direction of literary and elocution instructor Stella (or Ida) M. Case, as by this time, Vining was a popular booking at Chautauqua meetings around the country. In the cast were Vida Berry, Clarence Benedict, Clara Sherwood, Bert Samuel Stancliff, James Martin, Ernest Smith, Charles Logan, and Ernest Wright.

SOSNS students perform a tableau of Elizabeth Barrett Browning's "A Romance of the Ganges," a classic poem first printed in London in 1838 in *Finden's Tableaux: A Series of Picturesque Scenes of National Character, Beauty, and Costume*. The students portray the seven maidens standing by the Ganges River in the Barrett poem. The photograph was taken June 13, 1905, by Stella M. Case.

Alpha Tauri was formed as a student club to further dramatic work, and club members performed in college productions. Members pictured are, from left to right, (first row) Sylvia Greenleaf, Florence Stewart, Eleanor Brown, Faye Arthur (president), unidentified, Helen Lyons, and Elizabeth Morse; (second row) Wilma Howard, Marion Elizabeth Ady (adviser), Albie L. Beck, Riley Pittenger, Harry May, Verne V. Caldwell (adviser), John Churchman, William Pierce Tucker, Foss Cramer, and Lucille Calkins.

Angus Bowmer staged *The Merchant of Venice* and *Twelfth Night* on this stage at the 1935 Fourth of July celebration, considered the first performance of the Oregon Shakespeare Festival. The stage was hastily constructed on the site of Lithia Park's Chautauqua, and Works Progress Administration crews added a roof in 1936. The structure was destroyed by fire in 1940 and was rebuilt and expanded over the years. The university's relationship with the Oregon Shakespeare Festival has flourished for more than eight decades.

Papa Is All by Patterson Greene was the freshman play staged December 11–12, 1952. Performed in the round arena-style in the Churchill Hall auditorium, the show was directed by Mildred Peck, SONS speech instructor. The cast included Robene Starcher, Bob Hillyer, and Nancy Jennings, all of Medford; Esther Snook and Bert Simmons of Central Point; and Darrell Keeney of Roseburg.

Pictured is a 1959 art classroom showing molds, kiln, paints, and other supplies.

Hansel and Gretel was staged in April 1963 as a children's play directed by Dorothy Stolp and choreographed by Beverly Bennett. The Ashland and Medford branches of the American Association of University Women (AAUW) supported Southern Oregon College's children's theater productions for many years. Bennett was 1962–1963 AAUW Ashland president.

Marythea Grebner and Robert Alston are at a Britt Art Gallery exhibit in 1963 or 1964. Grebner began at SOSC in 1961 as an English instructor and was later director of Stevenson Union. In 1979, she was appointed to the Oregon Arts Commission to serve out Alice Sours's term, which expired in 1983. Robert Alston was hired to the art faculty in 1963; his abstract, vividly colored works were executed in oils.

The 1970s and 1980s saw new forms of art and music driven by cultural shifts and popular culture. This 1988 photograph shows a student at a weaving loom; courses were also added in ceramics and printmaking. A 10-member kazoo band played in 1978 accompanied by a masked cymbalist and a bubble blower.

Southern Oregon College music professor Fred Palmer conducts the Rogue Valley Symphony Orchestra in this 1970s-era photograph of the SOC Music Recital Hall in the Music Building. Palmer founded the symphony in 1967, and in 1976, SOC professor Ray Tumbelson founded the Rogue Opera. Max McKee was the symphony's musical director in the 1980s and 1990s; Martin Makjut has been maestro since 2010.

Margaret Evans often performed on this Balcom and Vaughan pipe organ installed in the Music Building's Music Recital Hall in 1974 thanks to the generosity and hard work of Agnes Flanagan and Worth Harvey. The organ has three manuals, four divisions, 29 stops, and 1,926 pipes. Flanagan and her husband's company, Elk Lumber, also made financial contributions to pipe organs at Lewis and Clark College, Portland, and First Presbyterian Church, Medford.

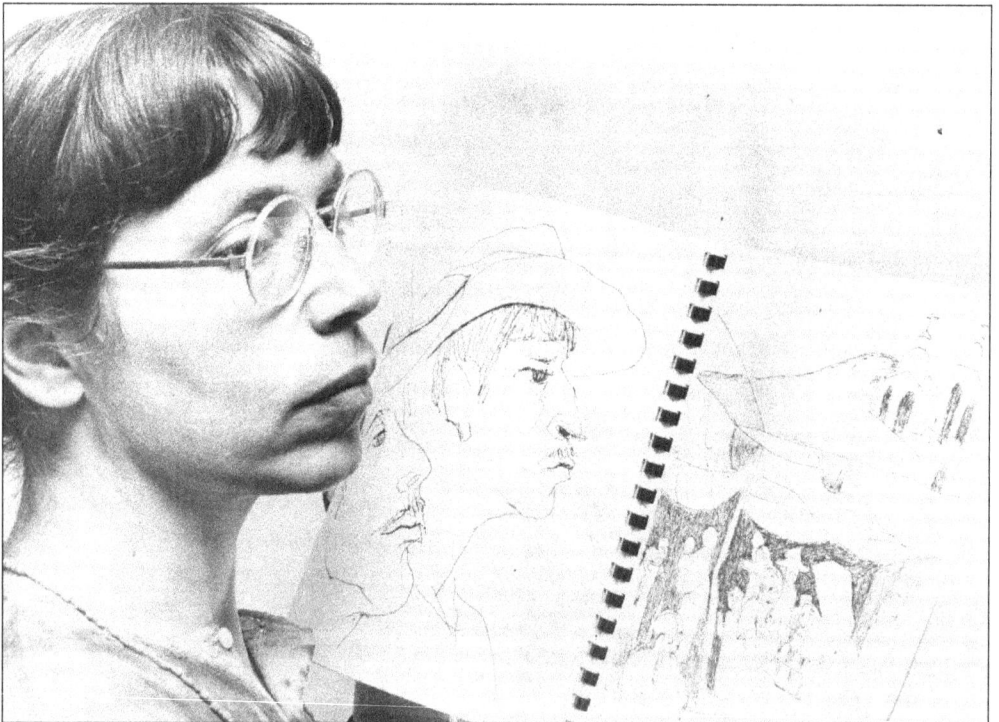

Influential artist, author, and activist Betty LaDuke taught in SOSC's art program from 1964 to 1996. LaDuke gained international recognition for her vivid photography, paintings, sketches, and murals based largely on social justice issues and women's experiences. Her works reflect travel to Asia, Africa, India, and Latin America, and more recently, her art has documented farmworkers' experiences in Southern Oregon as well as immigration concerns.

Composer Todd Barton was on the SOU music faculty from 1999 to 2010, and he was the Oregon Shakespeare Festival's resident composer from 1969 to 2012. Barton is known for his work with synthesizers, and his award-winning compositions have been performed around the world. In this 1980 image, Barton works with the Roland Jupiter-8 synthesizer and Serge Modular Music System. (Photograph by Christopher Briscoe.)

The faculty of the SOSC Art Department in 1980 includes, from left to right, (first row) Charles Edmonds, Clifford Sowell, Otto Wilda, and Frank Bedogne; (second row) Lyle Matoush (printmaking), Wesley Chapman (photography), James Doerter (art education), and Robert Alston (painting); Betty LaDuke is not in the photograph.

Craig Hudson (set design) and Elizabeth Adkisson (experimentation and interpretation) came to SOSC in 1978, when Dorothy Stolp retired from the theater department after 25 years. Hudson loved dinner theater, as did Stolp, and continued that tradition at SOU even after he opened the Oregon Cabaret Theatre with business partner Jim Giancarlo in 1986. In this 1988 photograph, Hudson (front) is constructing the set for *The Miser* at SOSC.

The Schneider Museum of Art has been an educational rite of passage for thousands of Southern Oregon children since it opened in 1986. Bill and Florence Schneider were major contributors to the museum, which is named after Bill's parents. This 1988 photograph was taken before the construction of the front patio and staircase, and the framing on the left outlines the art buildings that were not funded at the time.

Music student Terry Lund is on the trombone in this late 1980s photograph. In 2003, Lund won a Mr. Holland's Opus Award for Illinois Valley High School in Cave Junction and was also named an SOU Distinguished Alumnus.

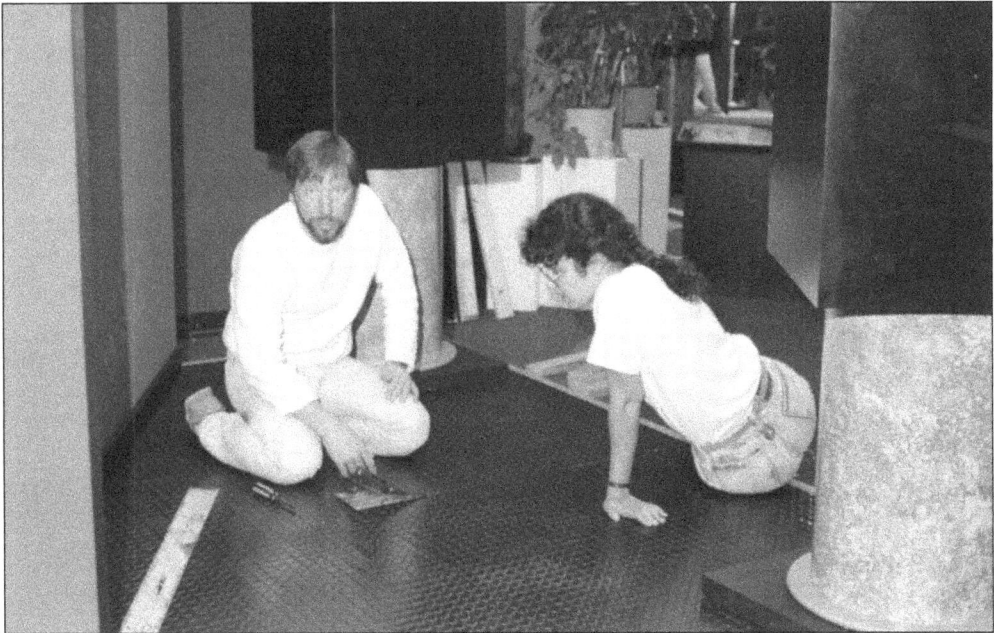

Alan Armstrong coordinated Shakespeare in Ashland: Teaching from Performance, the National Endowment for the Humanities–funded summer institutes for schoolteachers. Twenty-five high school teachers were selected for each four-week institute to study with Shakespeare scholars, master teacher Vince Wixon, and experts from the Oregon Shakespeare Festival. In this 1988 photograph, Armstrong is developing an exhibit for the lobby of the theater building. The institute ran from about 1983 through 2005.

Acclaimed poet Lawson Fusao Inada taught in SOU's English program from 1966 through 2002. Inada published three books of poetry and coedited two seminal anthologies of Asian American literature. His experiences as a child incarcerated in World War II internment camps are reflected in his poetry. In 2006, Inada was named Oregon's sixth poet laureate, a position he held through 2010. Inada's poetry and jazz have comforted, energized, and inspired many.

Kelly Kheen pins fabric and embellishments to a dress form as Michael Chapman, who taught directing and costume, looks on. Sewing goods are in the background. (Courtesy Chris Sackett.)

Paul French, pictured in 1990, is director of choral and vocal studies. He celebrated 30 years at Southern Oregon University in 2019. French also serves as artistic director and conductor for the Southern Oregon Repertory Singers. Ensembles under his direction have gained national and international recognition.

Professor and pianist Alexander Tutunov is a former first prize–winner of the Belarusian National Piano Competition and former winner of the Russian National Piano Competition. His recording of Abeliovich's Piano Concerto is featured on the Emmy Award–winning soundtrack of the History Channel series *Russia: Land of the Tsars*. Tutunov is the artistic director of the SOU International Piano Institute and was recently named the principal guest artist of the Port Angeles Symphony Orchestra.

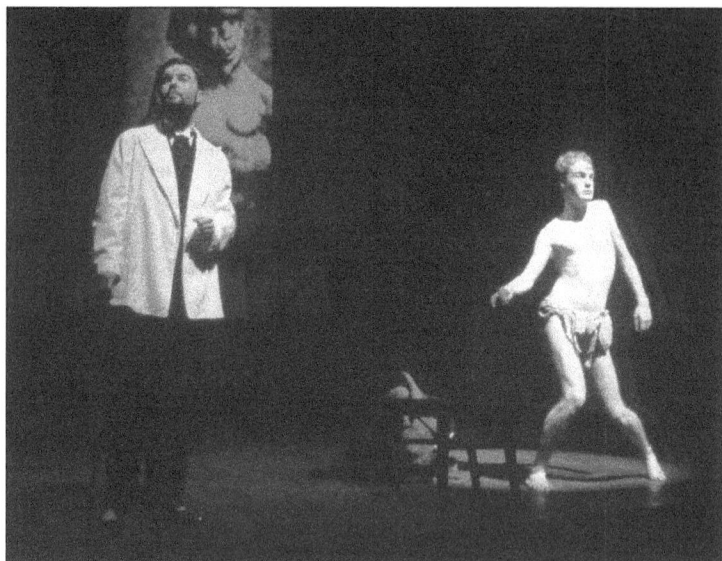

This still is from the 1999 production of *The Elephant Man*, with Kasey Mahaffy in the title role. Dennis Smith directed, Craig Hudson designed the set, Chris Sackett designed the lights, and Eyan Candini made the costumes. Hudson and Sackett worked more than two dozen shows between 1989 and 2001; Dale Luciano served as department chair from 1985 to 2000.

Construction of the Theater Arts Building was completed in 1982 at a cost of $3.8 million, with further renovation and expansion in 2018. The building now includes a wing for the Jefferson Public Radio facilities. The building houses the 325-seat Dorothy Stolp Center Stage Theater and the 125-seat black box theater. This image is from a 2016 production of Arthur Miller's *The Crucible*, directed by Oregon Shakespeare Festival director and actor James Edmonson.

Seven

REGIONALLY RESPONSIVE

Southern Oregon State College grew and transformed during the final decades of the last century. During the economic recession of the early 1980s and resultant cutbacks in the college's state-funded budgets, Dr. Natale Sicuro, who served as president from 1979 to 1987, directed attention to public and private fund-raising. The presidencies of Joe Cox, Stephen Reno, and Sara Hopkins-Powell were a time of growth and the cementing of a campus culture imbued with civility and inclusion.

President Sicuro's relationships with prospective donors, community organizations, and other public entities brought in significant funding that broadened opportunities for both students and the community. Principle examples include saving and renovating the historic Swedenburg House; replacing dilapidated bleachers with a modern multiuse stadium; constructing the Schneider Museum of Art; setting the stage to develop the North Campus along Ashland's East Main Street; encouraging donations to endow lectureships; and most importantly, stimulating increased giving for scholarships. Upon Sicuro's 1986 departure, Ernest Ettlich was appointed as interim president.

In 1987, Dr. Joseph Cox was appointed to replace Pres. Natale Sicuro. Under President Cox's leadership, academic programs were organized into four schools, and preprofessional programs were introduced in nursing, forest management, social work, and other disciplines. In 1994, he assumed interim chancellorship of the Oregon State System of Higher Education, and Provost Stephen Reno moved into the presidency, serving until 2000, when Dr. Sara Hopkins-Powell served as interim president for a year.

In 1997, SOSC attained university status with an official name change to Southern Oregon University. Major campus events during this time included the construction of the Theater Arts Building, KSOR's affiliation with National Public Radio, and construction of the Computing Services Center and family housing complex, which were both completed in 1990. The university began offering courses in Medford and expanded economic and educational services to the region.

During this era, the university's focus on inclusion and diversity became firmly entrenched in student life, regional outreach, and academic programs. The Women's Center expanded, the Queer Resource Center was established, and multicultural student unions flourished. The Annual Spring Powwow, first held in 1993, grew into one of the largest events on campus. Outreach programs like Konaway Nika Tillicum and Academia Latina began connecting to Native and Latino youth. The art, music, and theater programs flourished.

Grubbs Barn was located near Walker and East Main Streets, on SOU property known as the North Campus. For more than a century, Grubb's Barn and its ghost sign welcomed visitors to Ashland along the historic southern route of the Oregon Trail. The SOU Equestrian Club used the barn as a stable before it was removed for development in 1981. This later became the location of ScienceWorks Hands-On Museum. (Courtesy Terry Skibby.)

Natale Sicuro (left) was the university president from 1979 through 1986. He is pictured with then US vice president George H.W. Bush during his visit to Southern Oregon while campaigning on the Reagan-Bush ticket. President Sicuro left in 1986 to assume the presidency of Portland State University.

During both his 1984 and 1988 presidential campaigns, Jesse Jackson held rallies throughout Oregon, including Southern Oregon cities. In this photograph, Jackson is on campus during his 1984 campaign. He also spoke at the Jackson County Expo during his 1988 campaign and was back on campus to campaign for President Clinton in 1993.

Computers continued to change the world in the 1980s. Instead of punch cards to manage registration and student records and data tapes sent to Salem, desktop and network computers became available. At first, the secretarial program, made up mostly of women, trained on typewriters, and the new computer science program, largely men, used word processors with five-and-quarter-inch floppy disks. Lorraine Skaff-Winger taught in both programs. Paula Vincent is at the typewriter.

By 1988, the region needed workers who knew how to use personal computers and desktop software. SOU responded by building computer labs and graduating business and computer science students who could use the new equipment. The Suzuki Foundation and 3M in White City contributed financially and in kind to the growth of these programs.

In 1987, Dr. Joseph Cox was appointed to replace Natale Sicuro as president. President Cox (who has a doctorate in history from the University of Maryland) had most recently been vice president for academic affairs at Northern Arizona University. During his tenure at SOSC, academic programs were organized into four schools, and new academic programs were developed. President Cox left in 1994 to serve as interim chancellor of the Oregon State System of Higher Education.

This bearded man holding a hoedad is a student in the forest management preprofessional program. Tree planting was big business in Southern Oregon in the 1970s and 1980s, after massive clear-cuts harvested many acres of forestland. Experience and education demonstrated that native species, elevation, microclimate, and other factors would influence forest restoration. (Photograph by Christopher Briscoe.)

Hands-on learning 1980s-style is shown in this photograph of a math education class. Note the Venn diagram and game of Yahtzee in the photograph.

Students work on the 1983–1984 *Raider* yearbook under faculty adviser Tom Pyle (not pictured). The last yearbook was published in 1992. The full run of the *Raider* yearbooks, as well as Southern Oregon University's annual catalogs from 1878, is available online in the Southern Oregon Digital Archives.

SOU's mission of regional service was extended with the Elderhostel program, bringing visitors to campus where they stayed in dorms and went to the Oregon Shakespeare Festival. Local businesses sued SOU for unfair competition, and the Elderhostel program was transformed into a lifelong learning center that operates today as the Osher Lifelong Learning Institute (OLLI).

Radio producer John Baxter and his buddy Khayam the Cheetah are in this 1980s photograph. By then, SOU's KSOR radio broadcast initiative, led by Ron Kramer, was a National Public Radio affiliate, owned and operated 36 translators, and was the largest public radio network in the country. Programming was differentiated into three broadcast services thanks to the donation of several radio frequencies. In 1989, KSOR was renamed Jefferson Public Radio.

Mount Ashland has always been a winter destination for Southern Oregon State College students. Two sun-loving students take a break from their studies in this casual photograph. Southern Oregon State College managed the ski slopes at Mount Ashland for a time in the mid-1980s. (Photograph by Christopher Briscoe.)

When the Oregon National Guard considered relocating from Ashland and its historic armory on Oak Street, Natale Sicuro offered the Guard a long-term land lease on the SOU North Campus along East Main Street to keep it in the town. In this photograph, folks are looking up at a flyover in honor of the dedication; a football game was in progress at the time, and fans complained about the noise.

Ken Goddard, director of the National Fish and Wildlife Forensics Laboratory, is pictured in front of the almost completed lab constructed on Southern Oregon State College's North Campus in 1988. The National Fish and Wildlife Forensics Laboratory is the only one of its kind in the nation. Completing the East Main construction on the North Campus is a nonprofit museum constructed in 2001 and now known as ScienceWorks.

Jay Pegg earned a bachelor's degree in chemistry in the early 1990s. Here, he loads a sample into a cryomagnet for nuclear magnetic resonance spectroscopy.

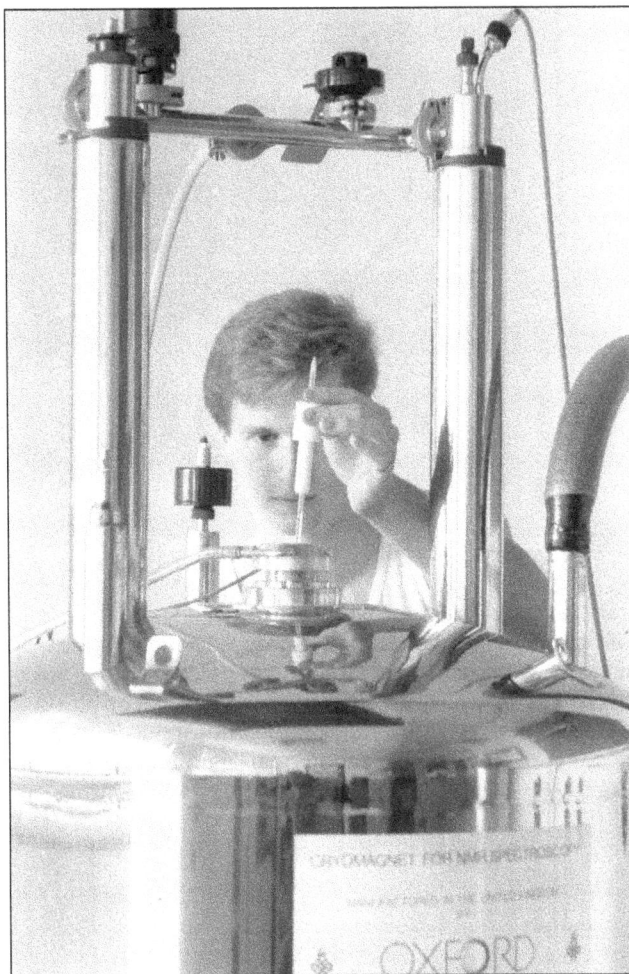

The Computing Services Center opened in the fall of 1990. The $3.2-million, 31,000-square-foot facility contains two wings. The east wing houses a student computer lab and two electronic classrooms, while the west wing houses administrative computing offices, academic offices, classrooms, a secure server room, and the campus telephone system hardware. (Courtesy Terry Skibby.)

The Old Mill Village student family housing complex of 130 apartments opened in 1990 between Wightman Street, California Street, Quincy Street, and the railroad. Phil Campbell, director of auxiliary services, oversaw land acquisition and construction. The community building located within the complex housed a childcare center, Laundromat, offices, and a meeting space. In 1997, an additional 35 units were added on the east side of Wightman Street.

This photograph from around 1992 shows Ron Bolstad, dean of administration, Pres. Joe Cox, and Provost Stephen Reno barbecuing for a crowd. Bolstad served at SOU for 22 years. Reno went on to assume the presidency of SOU in 1994, after Cox's departure to serve as interim chancellor of the Oregon State System of Higher Education.

In 1994, SOSC provost Stephen Reno moved into the presidency after Joe Cox's departure. President Reno served ably—setting a high standard for campus discourse and civility (Reno's doctoral work at UC Santa Barbara centered on religious studies)—until 2000, when he was appointed chancellor of the University System of New Hampshire. Upon President Reno's departure, Dr. Sara Hopkins-Powell served as interim president in 2000–2001.

Every summer, SOU hosts Konaway Nika Tillicum, an eight-day residential camp offering classes, lectures, cultural experiences, and recreational activities for Native American students completing grades 7–12. Konaway began in 1994 after a year of outreach to Oregon tribes to determine how SOU might best meet their educational needs. This innovative program that prepares students for higher education has become a model nationwide. Four Konaway participants are pictured here.

The Southern Oregon University Laboratory of Anthropology (SOULA) was formally established in the 1990s, but earlier SOU archaeologists had worked throughout the region. In this 2010 photograph, from left to right, SOULA archaeologists Mark Tveskov, Katie Johnson, and Chelsea Rose are excavating in Bandon. Working with the Coquille Indian tribe, this project helped city officials install underground utilities with minimal damage to both indigenous and settler archaeological remains.

Four Academia Latina students, participants in a summer academic residential program for Latino youth, are pictured here. The program offers a broad range of classes, lectures, cultural experiences, and recreational activities for Latino students who have completed grades 7–9. Academia Latina was created in 1999 to promote academic success among Latino youth of Southern Oregon.

Seven

A UNIVERSITY

FOR THE FUTURE

Since 2000, Southern Oregon University has seen unprecedented change. In 2001, Elisabeth Zinser became SOU president, serving through 2006. Dr. Mary Cullinan assumed SOU's presidency in 2006, leading SOU through state budget reductions and two painful retrenchments. Roy Saigo took over as interim president from 2014 to 2016, a critical post-retrenchment time when SOU transitioned to a new board of trustees. Effective July 1, 2015, state legislation abolished the Oregon University System, mandating that public universities establish institutional governing boards. SOU's 15-member board has broad authority to supervise and manage university affairs.

In the fall of 2016, immediately after assuming SOU's presidency during fiscally fraught times, Linda Schott led the campus through a two-year strategic planning process. The comprehensive final plan positions SOU to become the "University for the Future," focusing on transformative pedagogy, sustainability, financial viability, engagement beyond the campus, and equity, diversity, and inclusion.

SOU is creative and bold, as reflected in innovative academic programs like Outdoor Adventure Leadership and in campus enhancements such the new nine-hole disc golf course. Sustainability is a core SOU value and is reflected in the vitality of the Farm, the proliferation of solar panels, and being named the first Bee Campus USA.

Significant capital construction projects have transformed the campus. The four-building Center for the Visual Arts (CVA) complex was completed in 2000. The renovated and expanded Hannon Library, dedicated in 2005, doubled in size from 64,380 to 122,830 square feet. In 2008, SOU's Medford campus found a home in the new Higher Education Center (HEC), which it shares with Rogue Community College (RCC) in a unique partnership. Raider Village, located on the North Campus, opened in 2013 with residence halls and a dining commons. The 96,000-square-foot Lithia Motors Pavilion and adjacent Student Recreation Center opened in 2018, as did the expanded and renovated Theater Building and Jefferson Public Radio (JPR) Broadcast Center. Also in 2018, Thalden Pavilion became a new outdoor venue for education and performance at the Farm thanks to the generosity of Kathryn and Barry Thalden.

Southern Oregon University is poised to successfully navigate challenges facing higher education. Planning, innovation, and hard work position SOU to respond to changing demographics and regional needs and able to proactively establish programs and partnerships that ensure the university will flourish.

Two students are seated in the courtyard of the Center for the Visual Arts complex, which was completed in 2000. The four-building complex consolidated art programs. A new 19,000-square-foot Art Building houses ceramics, a 160-seat lecture hall, classrooms, seminar rooms, and galleries. The project included creation of the central courtyard and renovations to the DeBoer Sculpture Building, Marion Ady Building, and Schneider Museum of Art. (Photograph by Steve Babuljak.)

Elisabeth Zinser was SOU president from 2001 through 2006. She is pictured (center) with Cuauhtémoc Ojeda Rodríguez (left), rector of the University of Guanajuato, one of SOU's sister universities, and former SOU interim president Sara Hopkins-Powell. During President Zinser's presidency, SOU embarked on a strategic planning process based on the expertise of the National Center for Higher Education Management Systems that used budget-related decision-making tools.

The renovated and expanded Hannon Library was dedicated on May 18, 2005, doubling in size from 64,380 to 122,830 square feet. The award-winning building contains electronic classrooms, student computers, a coffee shop, a secure and climate-controlled special collections facility, fireplace alcoves, art galleries, meeting rooms, and 22 group study rooms. The soaring, glass-enclosed entrance rotunda features a mosaic by artists Robert Stout and Stephanie Jurs.

Pres. Mary Cullinan is meeting with Pres. Ki-hong Kwon of sister university Dankook University during a 2007 trip to South Korea. President Cullinan assumed the presidency in 2006 and led SOU through eight years of state budget reductions, enrollment fluctuation, campus construction, and new initiatives, including an honors college.

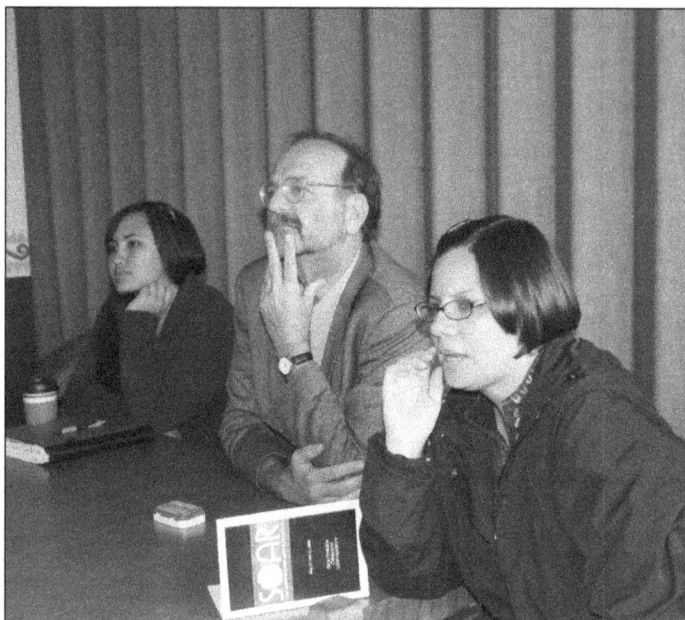

English faculty Alma Rosa Alvarez and Bill Gholson, along with an unidentified student, are listening to a Southern Oregon Arts and Research (SOAR) presentation. The first annual SOAR conference was held in May 2007. SOAR has provided opportunities for countless students, faculty, and staff to share their research and musical, dramatic, and artistic accomplishments. The weeklong program includes lectures, poster sessions, exhibits, and performances.

SOU's Medford campus is centered in the Higher Education Center at the corner of Eighth Street and Riverside Avenue. The 68,700-square-foot building, built to high environmental standards, opened in 2008. The HEC building is shared with Rogue Community College in a unique partnership and houses 29 classrooms, a lecture hall, a video conference room, a 100-seat presentation hall, science labs, computer labs, student study areas, and a café.

116

Native American studies director emeritus David West is pictured in 2012 with student Shawn Walker. Native American programs at SOU include a Native American studies minor and certificate program; outreach to Oregon tribes; Konaway Nika Tillicum, a residential summer camp for Native youth in grades 7–12; and an active Native American Student Union (NASU). For 25 years, NASU's annual spring powwow has been one of the largest events on campus.

Raider Village, located on the North Campus near the Lithia Motors Pavilion, opened in the fall of 2013 and contains two new residence halls and a dining hall. McLoughlin Hall features a suite design with single and double rooms, available as housing for junior and senior students. Shasta Hall is open to all students. The Hawk Dining Commons features stations with options for many dietary needs and preferences and houses a convenience store.

This aerial photograph highlights changes to SOU's North Campus with the 2013 completion of Raider Village, the residence hall complex, and the Hawk Dining Commons. McNeal Pavilion, the old gymnasium, is behind the new dormitories, with the Digital Media Center, which houses Rogue Valley Community Television (RVTV), to its right. McNeal Pavilion was demolished in 2016, making way for the new Lithia Motors Pavilion, completed in 2018. The SOU stadium can be seen at the top.

SOU president Roy Saigo (left) is pictured during a visit to Guanajuato with Dr. Carlos Torres Ramírez, secretary of the Guanajuato City Council. Roy Saigo was interim president from 2014 to 2016, a critical post-retrenchment time when SOU transitioned to a board of trustees. President Saigo is credited with helping stabilize enrollment and improve morale. Saigo's childhood experience in a World War II Japanese internment camp informed his commitment to diversity and inclusion.

Established by state legislation effective July 1, 2015, SOU's board of trustees has broad authority to manage university affairs. The board includes, from left to right, Steve Vincent, Lyn Hennion, Pres. Roy Saigo (ex officio), Dennis Slattery (faculty), April Sevcik (vice chair), Paul Nicholson, Jeremy Nootenboom (student), Joanna Steinman (staff), William D. Thorndike Jr. (chair), Teresa Sayre, and Judy Shih. Not pictured are Les AuCoin, Adam Washington, Filiberto Bencomo, and Sheri Bodager.

In the fall of 2016, immediately after assuming SOU's presidency during fiscally fraught times, Pres. Linda Schott led the campus through a comprehensive, inclusive two-year strategic planning process. Before coming to SOU, President Schott was president of the University of Maine at Presque Isle. A first-generation college student, Schott grew up on a Texas cattle ranch. She completed undergraduate work at Baylor University and her doctorate at Stanford University. (Photograph by Louise Rebel.)

The Outdoor Adventure Leadership (OAL) degree program is an example of SOU's bold, innovative academic programs. Offering degrees at graduate and undergraduate levels, OAL's integrated curriculum teaches transferable life and business skills through comprehensive coursework and internships. Expeditions in the SOU region, like the one in this photograph of Shane West rafting, and to remote areas of the world provide opportunities to develop skills as leaders, educators, and environmental stewards.

Student Shaun Franks (center) poses on solar panels with Roxane Beigel-Coryell, sustainability manager, and Dr. Vincent Smith (environmental studies). SOU's first solar array was placed on Hannon Library in 2000. More arrays were added during subsequent construction projects. In a major push during 2018–2019, three photovoltaic arrays were installed. SOU now has eight solar panel arrays on seven buildings, with total annual capacity of approximately 470,000 kilowatt hours of energy production.

Faculty member Jamie Hickner, who was instrumental in achieving SOU's Bee Campus USA designation, is tabling at Earth Day 2015, the year SOU was recognized as the first Bee Campus USA by Bee City USA, a national nonprofit. Following SOU's lead, there are now 60 designated Bee Campuses. SOU has created five pesticide-free pollinator gardens and incorporates native, pollinator-friendly plant species across campus whenever possible.

SOU alumnus Marvin Woodard Jr. is SOU's Multicultural Resource Center (MRC) coordinator, providing support and advising to multicultural student organizations. The MRC, located in Stevenson Union, supports African American, Latino/Hispanic American, Native American, Pacific Islander, American Asian, and queer communities at SOU. Woodard is a familiar figure at MRC events, whether the luau, salmon bake, or ribs barbecue.

121

Student farmer Amy Reynolds tends to spinach seedlings for the Farm. SOU's 5.5-acre farm at 155 Walker Street is maintained by student farmers and volunteers and produces healthy, sustainably harvested foods. In 2014, both the CSA (community-supported agriculture) program and weekly campus farm stand sales began. In 2018, the Thalden Pavilion was constructed on the Farm property as a venue for sharing outrageous innovation in sustainability through education and performance.

This is a photograph of Winter's a Drag 2017, a student-led drag performance. SOU's Queer Resource Center (QRC) has been active for over 30 years. SOU is nationally recognized as LGBTQ-friendly, ranking in *Campus Pride*'s Top 25 LGBTQ-friendly schools and *Choice College*'s 50 best colleges for LGBTQ students. In 2017, Affordable Colleges Online placed SOU seventh on its list of LGBTQ-friendly universities, noting SOU's gender-inclusive housing and Lavender Graduation.

SOU's Women's Resource Center was founded in 1976, during the feminist movement, and is still going strong. Riah Safady, the current WRC coordinator, is pictured on the left along with students and Pres. Linda Schott. The WRC provides a wide range of services, including advocacy, survivor support, educational outreach and prevention, a feminism library, and programming such as Sexpressions and the Feminist Fight Club events.

Ronald E. McNair scholar Cristian Ramirez graduated from Southern Oregon University in 2017 with a bachelor's of science in computer science and entered a graduate program in computer security at the University of Oregon. Cristian came to this country from Zacatecas, Mexico, at age eight. The Ronald E. McNair Postbaccalaureate Achievement Program was established at SOU in 2003 with federal funding to help students prepare for doctoral studies.

The 96,000-square-foot Lithia Motors Pavilion, which opened in 2018, was funded by a state bond and by donors, including $1 million from the DeBoer family and their company, Lithia Motors. The facility includes a gym that seats 1,400, classrooms, and rooms for training and sports medicine. (Photograph by Terry Skibby.)

Indigenous leader, author, and member of the International Council of 13 Indigenous Grandmothers Agnes Baker Pilgrim (Takelma) is pictured with Rocky the Raider at the 2018 opening of the new recreation center. A 1974 SOU graduate at age 50, she was named Distinguished Alumni of the Year in 2002. Affectionately known as Grandma Aggie, she was born in 1924 on the Siletz Indian Reservation. Her grandfather, George Harney, was chief during the Takelma removal from Southern Oregon.

SOU's expanded and renovated Theater Building and Jefferson Public Radio Broadcast Center was dedicated on November 10, 2018. The expansion and renovation adds 60,000 square feet, of which 7,000 is the JPR annex with state-of-the art broadcast studios. Total construction costs were $12.75 million. The Theater Building has new acting studios, control booths, a costume shop, a movement studio, a design studio, a lighting lab, and a green room.

Commencement! Every June, around 1,200 undergraduate and graduate students officially complete their academic programs at SOU. Commencement celebrates the graduates' hard work, future possibilities, and their official induction into the SOU Alumni Association. Until 2002, commencements were held at the band shell in Lithia Park; since 2003, commencement has been held on the athletic field at Raider Stadium.

BIBLIOGRAPHY

Almack, John C. "History of Oregon Normal Schools." *Quarterly of the Oregon Historical Society* 21, no. 2 (June 1920): 95–169.

Billings, Homer. Memories of the "Old Normal School" and the "Dark Ages" from 1909 to 1925 as recalled by Homer Billings (July 1958). Unpublished manuscript. University Archives, Southern Oregon University, Ashland.

Bornet, Vaughn Davis. *Leaders and Issues at Southern Oregon College, 1963 to 1980: A Reminiscence*. Talent, OR: Bornet Books, 2012.

Fifty Years: SOSC, 1926–1976, Golden Jubilee Alumni Magazine. Ashland: Southern Oregon State College Alumni Association, 1976.

Kreisman, Arthur. *Remembering: A History of Southern Oregon University*. Eugene: University of Oregon Press, 2002.

———. *Southern Oregon University: History of Our Buildings and Grounds*. Ashland: Southern Oregon University Office of Facilities Planning and Construction, 2004.

Leary, Kit, and Amy Richards. *Oregon Shakespeare Festival*. Charleston, SC: Arcadia Publishing, 2009.

McCall, Lydia. "A Brief History of Our School." *Normal Student* 5, No. 3 (November 1889): 1–2.

McNeal, Roy Wilson. *Southern Oregon College Cavalcade*. Ashland: Southern Oregon College Foundation, 1970.

Smith, Thomasine. *More than a Cookbook: Southern Oregon University Raider Club Edition*. Ashland: Southern Oregon University Raider Club, 1998.

Taylor, Arthur S. *Souvenir History of Southern Oregon College*. Ashland: Southern Oregon College, 1955.

Taylor, Arthur S., and Hugh G. Simpson. *A History of Southern Oregon College, 1872–1959*. Ashland: Southern Oregon College, 1959.

Tucker, William Pierce. "Ashland Normal School, 1869–1930 (In Two Parts, Part I)." *Oregon Historical Quarterly* 32, no. 1 (1931): 46–60.

———. "Ashland Normal School, 1869–1930 (In Two Parts, Part II)." *Oregon Historical Quarterly* 32, no. 2 (1931): 165–176.

Note: Many of these sources can be viewed online at: https://soda.sou.edu.

INDEX

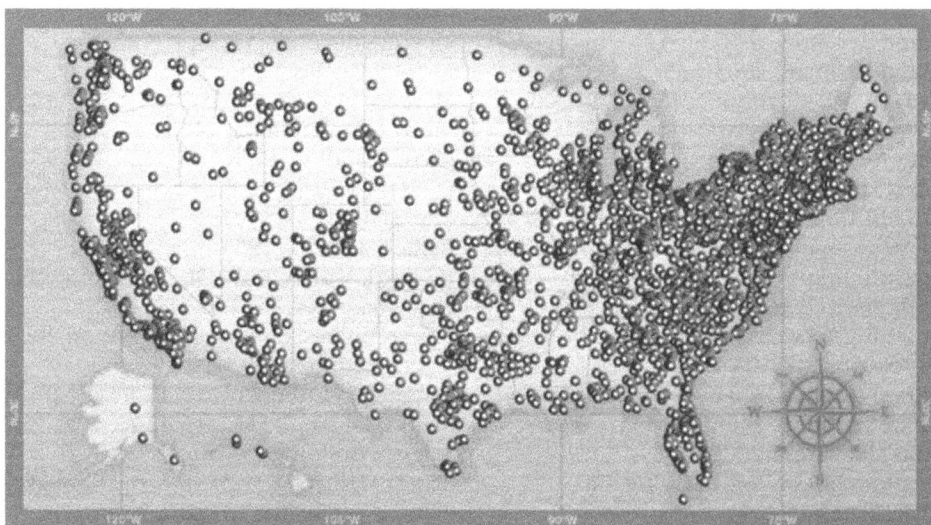

www.ingramcontent.com/pod-product-compliance
Lightning Source LLC
Chambersburg PA
CBHW080908100426
42812CB00007B/2205